MW00897247

BLACKSTONE OUTDOOR GAS GRIDDLE COOKBOOK

Discover 2000 Days of Delicious and Affordable Recipes to Master the Art of Griddle Cooking Year-Round and Improve Your Grilling Skills!

HUDSON BLAKE

Table of Contents

Introduction

Outdoor griddling has a rich history, evolving from humble campfires to sophisticated modern Outdoor griddling has a long history, starting from basic campfires to the high-tech Blackstone griddles we use today. It doesn't matter if you're a professional cook or just starting; cooking on a griddle is something special. The Blackstone Griddle, in particular, is a game-changer with its versatility, ease of use, and ability to bring out flavors that traditional cooking methods might miss. My motivation to write this cookbook stems from my deep love for outdoor cooking and the great memories I've created with family and friends around the griddle.

One of the main reasons I'm passionate about sharing these recipes is because I've discovered how this griddle can transform everyday meals into extraordinary culinary adventures. There's something magical about cooking outside; it's relaxing and invigorating at the same time. The sizzle of meat hitting the hot surface and the aroma wafting through the air makes every meal an event.

In this cookbook, I've compiled 2000 days' worth of recipes that cater to all tastes and occasions. From hearty breakfasts to delightful desserts, you'll find a wide variety of dishes that are not only delicious but also affordable. I believe good food shouldn't be expensive or complicated – it should be accessible to everyone.

Each recipe is designed with simplicity in mind. You won't need any fancy ingredients or complex techniques. Instead, you'll find step-by-step instructions that walk you through every part of the process. I wanted this cookbook to be like having a friend by your side, guiding you and sharing tips along the way.

Another motivation behind this book is to help you improve your grilling skills. Over time, you'll learn advanced techniques and tips that will elevate your cooking to new heights. From mastering searing and smoking to achieving the perfect steak doneness, every page is packed with valuable insights.

But this journey isn't just about individual recipes; it's also about embracing a lifestyle centered around food, community, and joy. Griddle cooking encourages us all to slow down and savor each moment – whether it's flipping pancakes for breakfast or grilling juicy burgers for dinner.

I hope this cookbook inspires you to fire up your Blackstone Griddle and start exploring new flavors. Remember, each recipe comes from my heart with the intent to make your outdoor cooking experience enjoyable and fun. Happy griddling!

History and Evolution of Outdoor Griddling

Outdoor cooking has always been a favorite pastime for many, with a history that goes back centuries. Initially, cooking outside started with simple campfires and evolved into more sophisticated methods as technology advanced. In the early days, people used open flames and rudimentary tools like skewers or pots to cook their meals outdoors. It was a way to bring communities together, share stories, and enjoy good food. As time went on, innovations in cooking technology began to take shape. The backyard barbecue became popular in the mid-20th century, marking a shift from open flames to charcoal grills. These grills offered more control over cooking temperatures and became a staple for family gatherings and summer cookouts. However, charcoal grilling had its downsides, such as uneven heating and lengthy preparation times.

The introduction of gas grills in the 1960s revolutionized outdoor cooking once again. Gas grills provided a quicker, more consistent heat source and eliminated many of the hassles associated with charcoal grilling. Fast forward to today, and we have an even better option: the outdoor gas griddle.

Enter the Blackstone Griddle, which represents the latest innovation in outdoor culinary equipment. Blackstone Griddles first hit the market in 2005 and have since grown in popularity due to their versatility and efficiency. Unlike traditional grills that have raised grates, griddles feature flat cooking surfaces that allow for even heat distribution. This means you can cook everything from pancakes to burgers without worrying about food falling through the cracks.

The evolution from open flame cooking to modern griddles like those from Blackstone signifies not only technological advancement but also an improvement in our outdoor cooking experiences. Today, Blackstone Griddles offer an unparalleled combination of convenience, performance, and versatility that caters to both novice cooks and seasoned chefs alike.

Benefits of Using a Blackstone Griddle

Now that we have a bit of history under our belts let's see why you should consider using a Blackstone Outdoor Gas Griddle in your own backyard or campsite, and why this piece of equipment stands out from other outdoor cooking options

1. **Ease of Use:** One of the standout features of Blackstone gas griddles is their user-friendly design. Whether you're a seasoned chef or just getting started with outdoor cooking, you'll find it simple to operate these griddles. Just connect it to a propane tank, ignite the burners, and you're ready to cook!
2. **Versatility:** Blackstone griddles are incredibly versatile. Their flat cooking surface allows you to prepare everything from breakfast staples like bacon and eggs to lunch favorites like burgers and sandwiches, and even dinner options like stir-fry or grilled vegetables. You can also easily make pancakes, quesadillas, or even pizzas on a Blackstone griddle.
3. **Even Cooking Surface:** Unlike traditional grills that have hot spots or uneven heat distribution, Blackstone griddles provide an evenly heated surface for consistent cooking results every time. This ensures that your food cooks uniformly without random burnt spots or undercooked areas.
4. **Portability:** Many models of Blackstone griddles are designed with portability in mind. They often come with wheels or detachable legs, making it easy to transport them for tailgating events, camping trips, or simply moving them around your backyard.
5. **Large Cooking Area:** Depending on the model you choose, Blackstone griddles offer ample space for cooking multiple items simultaneously – perfect for feeding large families or hosting gatherings with friends.

6. **Easy Clean-up:** Cleaning up after cooking is quick and hassle-free thanks to features like a built-in grease management system that collects drippings in one place for easy disposal. The flat surface also means there are no grills or grids where food can get stuck.
7. **Durability:** Constructed with high-quality materials like stainless steel burners and thick rolled steel surfaces, Blackstone griddles are built to last through many years of use. They are designed to withstand various weather conditions too when properly taken care of.

Getting Started with Your Blackstone Griddle

Unboxing and Assembling Your Griddle

When you first open the box, you'll find a collection of parts that may seem a bit overwhelming, but don't worry—it's simpler than it looks. Inside the box, you'll see the griddle top, the control panel, legs, shelves, and hardware needed for assembly. The first thing you'll need to do is carefully remove all these components from the box and place them on a flat surface.

Follow the user manual provided with your griddle as it will give you step-by-step instructions with illustrations. Generally, the process involves:

1. **Open the Box Carefully:** Place the box on a flat surface and cut the tape along the edges. Open the flaps and gently remove the contents.
2. **Check Contents:** Your Blackstone griddle should come with several key components:

   - ❑ The griddle top
   - ❑ The base unit
   - ❑ Burners

- ❑ Grease tray
- ❑ Propane tank holder (if applicable)
- ❑ Screws, bolts, and assembly tools
- ❑ Instruction manual

3. **Lay Out Everything:** Spread out all the components so you can see them clearly. This will make assembling much easier.
4. **Assemble the Base Unit:** Start by constructing the base unit as instructed in your manual. Typically, this involves connecting legs to a frame using provided screws and bolts.
5. **Attach Burners:** Securely attach the burners to the base unit, following the instructions carefully. Ensure they are fastened tightly, as this is critical for safety and function.
6. **Mount the Griddle Top:** Place the heavy griddle top onto the assembled base unit with caution. Make sure it is perfectly aligned and sits securely on top of the burners.
7. **Install Grease Tray:** Slide or attach the grease tray into its designated slot under or behind the griddle top.
8. **Propane Tank Setup:** If your model uses propane, connect your propane tank to the regulator valve according to manufacturer guidelines. Always check for leaks before lighting.

Congratulations! You've successfully assembled your Blackstone griddle. Now, let's move on to operating it.

Basic Operating Instructions

Now that your griddle is set up and looks impressive in your backyard or patio, it's time to get down to operating it. Here are some straightforward instructions to help you get started:

1. **Pre-checks:** Before you ignite your griddle for the first time, conduct some preliminary checks:
    a. *Gas Connection:* Ensure that your propane tank is properly connected. Always check for leaks by applying a soapy water solution around the connection area; if you see bubbles forming, tighten connections.
    b. *Burner Valves:* Make sure all burner knobs are in the "off" position before opening the gas line.

2. **Igniting Your Griddle:** Igniting a Blackstone griddle is simple:

    - Turn the propane tank valve counterclockwise to open it.
    - Push in and turn one of the burner knobs to start gas flow.
    - Press the igniter button while keeping the burner valve open until you hear a click and see flames.
    - Repeat this for other burners as needed based on what you're cooking.

3. **Preheating:** Once ignited, preheat your griddle by setting all burners to medium-high heat for about 10-15 minutes. This not only ensures even cooking but also helps maintain desired temperatures when grilling.
4. **Seasoning Your Griddle:** Before cooking for the first time (and periodically after), it's essential to season your griddle:

    - Apply a thin layer of cooking oil (vegetable oil or canola works well).
    - Spread it evenly across the surface using a paper towel—with caution as it'll be hot.
    - Allow oil to heat up and smoke off; this process creates a non-stick layer that's great for cooking.
    - Let it cool down and repeat the oiling/heating process 2-3 times.

5. **Temperature Control:** One of the benefits of a gas griddle is precise temperature control:

    a. *High Heat (400°F-500°F):* Ideal for searing meats like steaks and burgers.
    b. *Medium Heat (300°F-400°F):* Perfect for cooking vegetables, poultry, or fish.
    c. *Low Heat (200°F-300°F):* Great for cooking delicate items like eggs or keeping food warm.

You can adjust each burner individually based on what you're cooking.

6. **Basic Techniques:** Using a griddle is simple once you know some basic techniques:

    a. *Direct Searing:* Use high heat directly under the food for quick searing.
    b. *Indirect Cooking:* For thicker cuts of meat, use medium heat and close the lid (if provided) to cook food more evenly.
    c. *Stir-Frying:* Maintain medium-high heat while continuously stirring vegetables or meats to cook evenly without burning.

Daily Maintenance Tips

Taking care of your griddle every day is easier than you might think, and it really helps it last longer and work better. After you've seasoned your griddle, it's all about maintenance.

1. **Cool Down:** Always let the griddle cool down to a safe temperature before cleaning.
2. **Scrape Off Food Debris:** Use a spatula or scraper to remove any leftover food particles on the surface.
3. **Wipe Clean:** After scraping off food debris, wipe down the surface with a paper towel or cloth.
4. **Apply Oil:** Lightly coat your griddle with cooking oil after each use to maintain its non-stick surface and prevent rust.
5. **Store Properly:** If you're not planning to use your griddle for an extended period, make sure it's stored in a dry location and cover it to protect against dust and moisture.

Deep Cleaning Tips

Occasionally, your griddle will need a more thorough cleaning to keep it performing its best:

1. **Steam Cleaning:** While the griddle is still warm (but not hot), pour some water on the surface and let it steam up. Use a spatula or scraper to remove any stuck-on food debris more effectively.
2. **Soap Cleaning:** If you notice heavy residue buildup that regular cleaning doesn't remove, you might need to use soap again. Remember to re-season your griddle after using soap since it can strip away your seasoning layer.

Essential Tools and Accessories for Every Griddler

Whether you're a novice or a seasoned pro, having the right tools and accessories can make all the difference when cooking on your Blackstone Outdoor Gas Griddle. Let's explore the must-haves and nice-to-haves to elevate your grilling game to new heights. Let's dive in!

The Must-Haves

1. **Spatulas and Scrapers**

    a. *Long, Wide Spatula:* Perfect for flipping burgers, pancakes, and anything else you cook on your griddle.

    b. *Grill Scraper:* Essential for cleaning the griddle surface. It helps in scraping off stubborn food residue.

2. **Oil Container**

    a. *Squeeze Bottle:* Very handy for quick greasing of the griddle surface with oil. Keeps things neat and avoids spills.

3. **Tongs:** A sturdy pair of tongs are invaluable for handling hot dogs, sausages, vegetables, and more without piercing them, which helps retain juices.
4. **Meat Thermometer:** Ensures your meat is cooked to perfection every time. No more guessing if that chicken is fully cooked!
5. **Basting Cover:** Great for melting cheese on burgers or steaming vegetables under it by trapping steam within.
6. **Squirt Bottles:** For water to manage flare-ups or for adding that quick splash of soy sauce or other liquids without making a mess.
7. **Cutting Board:** A durable surface to prep your ingredients near your griddle.
8. **Knife Set:** Sharp knives are essential for chopping and prepping your ingredients efficiently.

The Nice-to-Haves

1. **Warming Rack:** Convenient for keeping your food warm while other items continue to cook.
2. **Chopping Mats:** Flexible mats make transferring chopped food onto the griddle easier.

3. **Burger Press:** Ensures evenly shaped burgers every time.
4. **Melting Dome:** Similar to a basting cover but often with a handle—excellent for ensuring even heat distribution when cooking.
5. **Grill Weights/Presses:** Useful for pressing down on bacon or sandwiches to ensure even cooking.
6. **Additional Storage Solutions:** Hooks or magnetic strips can be attached to keep your tools nearby, organized, and easily accessible.
7. **Heat Resistant Gloves:** Protects your hands from high heat when adjusting foods or cleaning the grill while it's still hot.
8. **Wind Guards:** Helpful in maintaining consistent temperature control if you're grilling in a windy area.

The Cool Extras

1. **Grill Mats/Sheets:** Non-stick mats that make cleaning up a breeze while preventing small bits of food from falling through any gaps.
2. **BBQ Grill Light:** Attach it directly to your griddle; perfect for those late-night grilling sessions when visibility is not optimal.
3. **Digital Timer:** Keeping track of multiple items grilling at different times can be tricky; a digital timer simplifies this task.
4. **Tool Organizer Caddy:** Keeps all your brushes, spatulas, and scrapers organized in one convenient place.

Advanced Techniques and Tips of Gas Griddle Cooking

Advanced Cooking Techniques: From Searing to Smoking

Knowing advanced cooking techniques helps you get the most out of your cooking equipment and makes your food taste amazing. By mastering these advanced skills, you'll be able to impress your friends and family with restaurant-quality meals right in your backyard. Plus, it makes cooking more enjoyable and rewarding when you know you're using the best methods to get great results every time.

Searing

Searing is all about locking in flavor. This technique involves cooking the surface of your food—usually meat—at a high temperature until it turns brown and forms a delicious crust. Here's how to do it:

1. **Preheat Your Griddle:** Turn your Blackstone griddle to high heat. Let it preheat for about 10 minutes until it's screaming hot.
2. **Prepare Your Meat:** While the griddle is heating, pat your meat dry with paper towels. Season with salt and pepper or any rub you prefer.

3. **Add Oil:** Once the griddle is hot, add a thin layer of high smoke point oil like vegetable or canola.
4. **Sear the Meat:** Place your meat on the griddle, pressing slightly to ensure full contact with the surface. Don't move it around; let it sit for 2-3 minutes.
5. **Flip Once:** After you've achieved a beautiful brown crust, flip the meat and sear the other side for another 2-3 minutes.
6. **Finish Cooking:** Depending on the cut and desired doneness, you might need to turn down the heat and cook a bit longer.

Use a thermometer to check internal temperatures for doneness:

- **Rare:** 120-130°F
- **Medium Rare:** 130-135°F
- **Medium:** 140-150°F
- **Well Done:** 160°F+

Smoking

Yes, you read that right! You can indeed smoke food on a gas griddle using a smoker box or simply wrapping wood chips in aluminum foil. Though traditionally done in smokers, you can achieve this on your Blackstone griddle with a bit of creativity.

1. **Set Up Two Zones:** Create two heat zones on your griddle—one side on high heat and one on low or off.
2. **Use Wood Chips:** Soak wood chips in water for about 30 minutes. Drain them and wrap tightly in aluminum foil with perforated holes on top.
3. **Place Wood Chips:** Put this foil packet directly over the high heat zone until it starts smoking.
4. **Place Food on the Cool Zone:** Place whatever you're smoking (meat, veggies) on the cool side of the griddle away from direct heat.
5. **Cover and Smoke:** Use a large metal lid or aluminum pan over your food to trap in the smoke.
6. **Low and Slow:** Maintain low temperature (225°F-250°F) by occasionally adjusting zones if needed and let it cook slowly, absorbing all that smoky goodness.

COMMON WOODS FOR SMOKING AND THEIR FLAVOR PROFILES		
WOOD TYPE	**FLAVOR PROFILE**	**BEST WITH**
Apple	Sweet, Fruity	Pork, Poultry
Mesquite	Strong, Earthy	Beef, Lamb
Hickory	Rich, Bacon-like	Pork Ribs, Bacon
Cherry	Mild, Fruity	Chicken, Turkey
Oak	Medium, Nutty	Beef Brisket

Mastering Indirect Cooking: Beyond the Basics

Indirect cooking means placing your food away from direct flame or heat source. Unlike direct cooking, where food sits right above the flame, indirect cooking allows heat to circulate around the food, which cooks it slowly and evenly. This method is especially useful for larger cuts of meat, delicate items like fish, or when you want to avoid burning the exterior while ensuring the interior is thoroughly cooked. You might be wondering how to set up a flat griddle for indirect cooking since there aren't any obvious sides with different temperatures. Here's how you do it:

1. **Preheat the Griddle:** First, set all burners to medium-high heat for 10-15 minutes to get the griddle very hot.
2. **Turn Off Some Burners:** After preheating, turn off one or more burners. The area directly above these burners will now be cooler and act as your "indirect" zone.
3. **Adjust Flame Levels:** Keep the remaining burners at medium to create a steady and even heat on the rest of the griddle.

ZONE TYPE	TEMPERATURE	USES
Hot Zone	450°F - 500°F	Searing and browning
Cool Zone	225°F - 250°F	Slow cooking and smoking

This setup will provide you with both hot and cooler zones on your griddle, allowing you to cook different types of foods simultaneously.

To make sure you get the best out of indirect cooking on your Blackstone griddle, follow these practical tips:

1. **Use a Lid or Dome Cover:** Covering your food with a lid or dome can help trap heat and moisture, making up for the lack of a conventional grill lid.

2. **Utilize Water Pans:** Placing a water pan in the indirect zone can help moderate temperature and add moisture to the air around your food.
3. **Temperature Monitoring:** Always use a meat thermometer to ensure that larger cuts of meat reach safe internal temperatures without overcooking.
4. **Oil Management:** Brush oil only in areas where you're placing food directly; otherwise too much oil can cause flare-ups even in indirect zones.

IDEAL TEMPERATURE RANGES FOR INDIRECT COOKING		
FOOD	**TEMPERATURE**	**NOTES**
Chicken (Whole)	165°F	Juicy and safe
Pork Shoulder	195°F	Tender and shreddable
Fish	145°F	Flaky but moist
Ribs	190-203°F	Fall-off-the-bone
Beef Brisket	200°F	Melts in your mouth

Steak Doneness: Achieving the Perfect Cook Every Time

Steak doneness refers to how thoroughly a steak is cooked. There are five main levels of doneness: rare, medium-rare, medium, medium-well, and well-done. Each level has its own texture, flavor, and juiciness.

DONENESS LEVEL	INTERNAL TEMPERATURE	NOTES
Rare	120-130°F	Cool red center; very soft and tender.
Medium-Rare	130-135°F	Warm red center; firm yet still very juicy.
Medium	135-145°F	Warm pink center; more firm and flavorful.
Medium-Well	145-155°F	Slightly pink center; firmer and less juicy.
Well-Done	155°F+	Brown throughout; very firm with minimal juices.

Cooking steak to your preferred doneness isn't just about timing – it's about having the right tools. Here's what you'll need:

1. **A meat thermometer:** This is essential for checking internal temperatures.
2. **Good quality tongs:** For flipping your steaks without piercing them.
3. **A timer:** Helps keep track of cooking times more accurately.

Cooking Tips for Perfect Steak Doneness

1. **Choosing the Right Steak Cut:** Before we get cooking, remember that not all steak cuts are equal. Cuts like ribeye, sirloin, filet mignon, and T-bone have different thicknesses and marbling (fat distribution), affecting how they cook. Choose a cut that suits your taste and budget.
2. **Sear It Right:** Place the steak on the hot griddle and let it sear for about 2-3 minutes without moving it. This creates a delicious crust.
3. **Flip It Over:** Flip the steak using tongs (not a fork – you don't want to pierce the meat). Sear the other side for another 2-3 minutes.
4. **Monitoring Temperature:** Insert the thermometer into the thickest part of the steak. Compare the temperature reading with our doneness table above. Remember that meat continues to cook slightly after being removed from heat (carryover cooking), so aim for a few degrees below your target temp.
5. **Resting Period:** Once it hits the desired temperature, remove the steak from the griddle and let it rest for about 5 minutes under tented aluminum foil. This helps redistribute juices throughout the meat.

Breakfast on the Griddle

1. Breakfast Bagel Bites

Prep time	Cooking time	Servings
10 mins	15 mins	6

Ingredients:

- 3 plain bagels, halved
- 6 large eggs
- 1 cup shredded cheddar cheese
- 1/2 cup cooked bacon bits
- 1/4 tsp salt
- 1/4 tsp black pepper
- 2 tbsp butter

Tips: You can substitute bacon with cooked sausage crumbles or ham for variation.

Serving size: 1 bagel bite

Nutritional values (per serving): Calories: 320; Fat: 18g; Carbs: 26g; Protein: 15g

Directions:

1. Preheat your griddle to medium heat. Melt the butter on the hot griddle. Place bagel halves cut side down and lightly toast for 2 minutes. Set aside.
2. In a bowl, whisk together eggs, salt, and black pepper. Pour it onto the griddle and scramble until fully cooked.
3. Assemble bagel halves with scrambled eggs, bacon bits, and cheese on top. Close the griddle cover to melt the cheese for 2 minutes. Serve warm.

2. Golden French Toast with Fresh Berries

Prep time	Cooking time	Servings
10 mins	10 mins	4

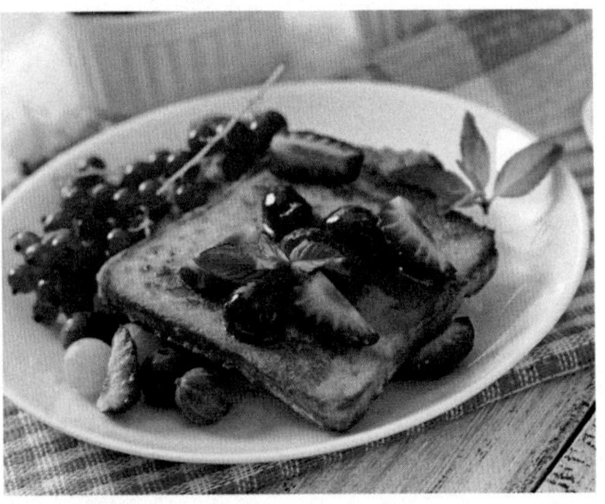

Ingredients:

- 1 cup milk
- 2 large eggs
- 1 tsp vanilla extract
- 1/2 tsp ground cinnamon
- 1 tbsp butter
- 8 slices bread
- 1 cup fresh berries
- Maple syrup for serving

Tips: Use day-old bread for better absorption of the egg mixture.

Serving size: 2 slices

Nutritional values (per serving): Calories: 260; Fat: 10g; Carbs: 35g; Protein: 8g

Directions:

1. Preheat your griddle to medium heat. In a bowl, whisk together milk, eggs, vanilla extract, and cinnamon. Melt the butter on the griddle.
2. Dip each slice of bread into the milk mixture, coating both sides evenly. Place the bread slices on the griddle and cook for 3-4 minutes per side until golden brown.
3. Serve topped with fresh berries and a drizzle of maple syrup.

3. Breakfast Skillet with Sausage and Potatoes

Prep time	Cooking time	Servings
15 mins	20 mins	4

Ingredients:

- 4 whole English muffins
- 8 oz smoked salmon slices
- 1/2 cup cream cheese
- 1 tbsp capers (optional)

Tips: Use pre-cooked sausage to save time on cooking. Slice potatoes thinly for quicker cooking.

Serving size: 2 cups

Nutritional values (per serving): Calories: 350; Fat: 20g; Carbs: 30g; Protein: 15g

Directions:

1. Preheat your griddle to medium-high heat. Add olive oil to the griddle, then add potatoes and cook for 10 minutes until they start to soften.
2. Add sausage and cook until browned, breaking it up as it cooks. Add bell peppers and onions, then sauté for another 5 minutes until vegetables are tender.
3. Mix all ingredients together and season with salt and pepper. Serve.

4. Mushroom and Spinach Frittata

Prep time	Cooking time	Servings
10 mins	15 mins	4

Ingredients:

- 1 cup sliced mushrooms
- 1 cup fresh spinach leaves
- 6 large eggs
- 1/4 cup milk
- 1/4 cup grated Parmesan cheese
- 2 tbsp olive oil
- Salt and pepper to taste

Tips: Serve with a side salad for a complete meal.

Serving size: 1 wedge

Nutritional values (per serving): Calories: 180; Fat: 13g; Carbs: 3g; Protein: 12g

Directions:

1. Preheat the outdoor gas griddle to medium heat. In a bowl, whisk together the eggs, milk, Parmesan cheese, salt, and pepper.
2. Add olive oil to the griddle and sauté the mushrooms for 5 minutes until tender. Add spinach and cook for 2 minutes until wilted.
3. Pour the egg mixture over the mushrooms and spinach. Cook for 7 minutes until the eggs are set but still slightly runny on top.
4. Flip the frittata and cook for an additional 2-3 minutes until fully set. Remove, cut into wedges, and serve immediately.

5. English Muffins with Smoked Salmon

Prep time	Cooking time	Servings
10 mins	N/A	2

Ingredients:

- 3 plain bagels, halved
- 6 large eggs
- 1 cup shredded cheddar cheese
- 1/2 cup cooked bacon bits
- 1/4 tsp salt
- 1/4 tsp black pepper
- 2 tbsp butter

Tips: For extra flavor, you can add a squeeze of lemon juice over the smoked salmon before serving.

Serving size: Half an English muffin with toppings

Nutritional values (per serving): Calories: 210; Fat: 13g; Carbs: 15g; Protein: 11g

Directions:

1. Preheat the outdoor gas griddle to medium heat. Split the English muffins in half and place them on the griddle, cut side down. Toast for 3-4 minutes or until golden brown.
2. Spread some cream cheese on each toasted English muffin half. Layer slices of smoked salmon over the cream cheese. Sprinkle capers on top if using, then serve.

6. Bacon and Egg Breakfast Burritos

Prep time	Cooking time	Servings
15 mins	10 mins	4

Ingredients:

- 4 large flour tortillas
- 8 large eggs
- 1 cup shredded cheddar cheese
- 1 cup cooked bacon bits
- 1/2 cup diced onions
- 1/2 cup diced bell peppers
- Salt and pepper to taste

Tips: For added flavor, you can include a tablespoon of salsa inside each burrito.

Serving size: 1 burrito

Nutritional values (per serving): Calories: 350; Fat: 20g; Carbs: 28g; Protein: 25g

Directions:

1. Preheat your outdoor gas griddle to medium heat.
2. Cook bacon bits on the griddle until crispy, then remove and set aside. Sauté onions and bell peppers on the griddle until they are softened.
3. In a bowl, whisk eggs with salt and pepper, then pour egg mixture onto the griddle with onions and peppers. Scramble eggs until fully cooked, then mix in bacon bits.
4. Warm tortillas on the griddle for about a minute per side. Add scrambled egg mixture to each tortilla, sprinkle with cheddar cheese, then roll into burritos.

7. Blueberry Pancakes with Maple Syrup

Prep time	Cooking time	Servings
10 mins	15 mins	4

Ingredients:

- 1 cup all-purpose flour
- 1 tbsp sugar
- 1 tsp baking powder
- 1/2 tsp baking soda
- 1/4 tsp salt
- 3/4 cup buttermilk
- 1 large egg
- 1 cup fresh blueberries
- Maple syrup for serving

Tips: Do not overmix the batter; a few lumps are fine.

Serving size: 2 pancakes

Nutritional values (per serving): Calories: 210; Fat: 6g; Carbs: 34g; Protein: 6g

Directions:

1. Preheat your outdoor gas griddle to medium heat. In a bowl, whisk together flour, sugar, baking powder, baking soda, and salt.
2. In another bowl, combine buttermilk and egg, then whisk until smooth. Combine it with dry mixture until blended. Fold in blueberries.
3. Grease the griddle with a small amount of oil or butter. Pour batter onto the griddle to form pancakes of desired size.
4. Cook for 2-3 minutes until bubbles form on the surface; flip and cook for another 2 minutes or until golden brown. Serve hot with maple syrup.

8. Corned Beef Hash and Fried Eggs

Prep time	Cooking time	Servings
10 mins	15 mins	4

Ingredients:

- 1 lb. canned corned beef, diced
- 2 cups frozen diced potatoes
- 1 small onion, chopped (optional)
- Salt and pepper to taste
- 2 tbsp vegetable oil
- 4 large eggs

Tips: Make sure corned beef is well-cooked for added crispiness.

Serving size: 1 egg with a portion of hash

Nutritional values (per serving): Calories: 310; Fat: 20g; Carbs: 15g; Protein: 16g

Directions:

1. Preheat your outdoor gas griddle to medium-high heat. Add oil and let it heat up slightly. Spread potatoes on one side of the griddle. Cook for 7 minutes or until they start to brown.
2. Add diced corned beef and onion to the potatoes, stirring occasionally for 7 minutes until everything is crispy. Season with salt and pepper.
3. On another section of the griddle, crack eggs directly onto the surface and cook to desired doneness. Serve eggs on top of corned beef hash.

9. Eggs In a Basket

Prep time	Cooking time	Servings
5 mins	10 mins	4

Ingredients:

- 4 slices of bread
- 4 eggs
- 2 tbsp butter
- Salt and pepper to taste

Tips: Use thick slices of bread for best results. Top with grated cheese, if desired.

Serving size: 1 slice with egg

Nutritional values (per serving): Calories: 200; Fat: 12g; Carbs: 15g, Protein: 8g

Directions:

1. Preheat the outdoor gas griddle to medium heat. Use a round cookie cutter or the rim of a glass to cut out the center of each bread slice.
2. Spread butter on both sides of the bread slices and the cut-out circles. Place the bread slices and circles on the griddle and cook for 1-2 minutes until golden brown.
3. Flip the bread over and crack an egg into each hole. Cook for another 3-4 minutes, until the eggs reach your desired doneness. Season with salt and pepper.

10. Loaded Breakfast Pizza

Prep time	Cooking time	Servings
15 mins	10 mins	4

Ingredients:

- 1 lb. pizza dough
- 6 eggs
- 1 cup shredded cheddar cheese
- 1 cup cooked bacon, chopped
- 1/2 cup green bell pepper, chopped

Tips: Use pre-cooked dough for a quicker process. Add your favorite breakfast toppings like sausage or mushrooms.

Serving size: 2 slices

Nutritional values (per serving): Calories: 420; Fat: 25g; Carbs: 30g; Protein: 18g

Directions:

1. Preheat the outdoor gas griddle to medium-high heat. Roll out pizza dough to desired thickness and shape on a floured surface.
2. Place dough on griddle and cook for 5 minutes until bubbles form on top. Flip the dough, then top with cheese, cooked bacon, bell pepper, and crack eggs over the top evenly spaced.
3. Cover and cook for another 7 minutes, until eggs are set. Season with salt and pepper.

11. Huevos Rancheros Breakfast Bowls

Prep time	Cooking time	Servings
10 mins	15 mins	4

Ingredients:

- 2 cups salsa
- 1 cup black beans, drained and rinsed
- 4 large eggs
- 1 cup shredded cheddar cheese
- 2 tbsp olive oil
- 4 small tortillas
- 1/4 cup chopped cilantro

Tips: Warm up tortillas until slightly crispy for added texture. Add a slice of avocado for extra creaminess.

Serving size: 1 bowl

Nutritional values (per serving): Calories: 320; Fat: 18g; Carbs: 29g; Protein: 15g

Directions:

1. Preheat your outdoor gas griddle to medium-high heat. Heat the olive oil on the griddle and cook the salsa and black beans for 3 minutes.
2. Push the salsa and beans to one side of the griddle and warm the tortillas on the other side. Crack the eggs directly onto the griddle and cook to desired doneness.
3. Assemble each bowl with a warm tortilla, beans, salsa, an egg on top, and sprinkle with cheddar cheese and cilantro.

12. Buttermilk Biscuits and Gravy

Prep time	Cooking time	Servings
10 mins	20 mins	4

Ingredients:

- 2 cups self-rising flour
- 1/2 cup cold butter, cubed
- 3/4 cup buttermilk
- 1 lb. breakfast sausage
- 2 cups milk
- 2 tbsp flour
- Salt and pepper to taste

Tips: For fluffier biscuits, do not over-knead the dough. Use spicy sausage for added flavor.

Serving size: 5 biscuits with gravy

Nutritional values (per serving): Calories: 525; Fat: 35g; Carbs: 38g; Protein: 18g

Directions:

1. Preheat your outdoor gas griddle to medium heat. In a bowl, cut butter into self-rising flour until pea-sized crumbles form. Slowly add buttermilk until dough forms.
2. Roll out dough on floured surface, cut into biscuits using a round cutter. Cook biscuits on the griddle for 5 minutes each side until golden brown.
3. In a skillet on the griddle, cook sausage until browned. Sprinkle in flour and mix well.
4. Gradually whisk in milk, cook until gravy thickens. Season with salt and pepper. Serve biscuits topped with sausage gravy.

Vegetables and Side Dishes

13. Grilled Vegetable Skewers with Herb Marinade

Prep time	Cooking time	Servings
15 mins	15 mins	6

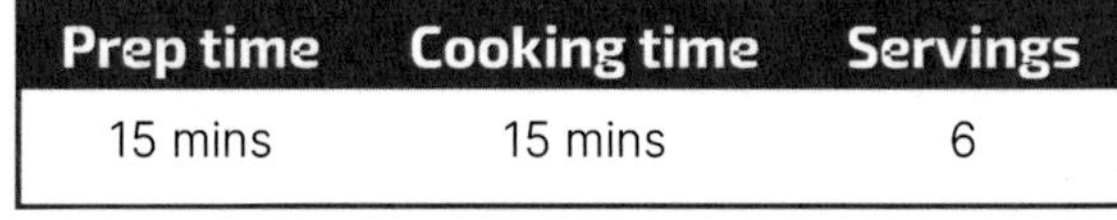

Ingredients:

- 1 cup cherry tomatoes
- 1 cup bell peppers (red, yellow, green), cut into chunks
- 1 cup zucchini, sliced into rounds
- 1 red onion, cut into chunks
- 2 tbsp olive oil
- 2 tbsp fresh parsley, chopped
- 1 tsp dried oregano
- 1 tsp dried thyme

Tips: For added flavor, squeeze a bit of lemon juice over the vegetables just before serving.

Serving size: 1 skewer

Nutritional values (per serving): Calories: 70; Fat: 4g; Carbs: 8g; Protein: 2g

Directions:

1. Preheat the outdoor gas griddle to medium-high heat. In a bowl, whisk together olive oil, parsley, oregano, and thyme.
2. Thread cherry tomatoes, bell peppers, zucchini, and red onion onto skewers. Brush the vegetable skewers evenly with the herb marinade.
3. Place the skewers on your griddle and cook for 15 minutes, turning occasionally until vegetables are lightly charred.

14. Caramelized Onion and Tomato Tart

Prep time	Cooking time	Servings
10 mins	20 mins	4

Ingredients:

- 1 cup cherry tomatoes, halved
- 2 large onions, thinly sliced
- 1 sheet puff pastry
- 2 tbsp olive oil
- 1 tsp salt
- 1 tsp black pepper
- 1 tbsp balsamic vinegar

Tips: Keep an eye on the caramelizing process to prevent burning. You can add fresh basil for extra flavor.

Serving size: 1 square

Nutritional values (per serving): Calories: 250; Fat: 15g; Carbs: 25g; Protein: 4g

Directions:

1. Heat the outdoor gas griddle to medium heat. Add olive oil and onions to the griddle. Cook for 10 minutes until onions are caramelized.
2. Add cherry tomatoes and cook for another 5 minutes. Drizzle with balsamic vinegar and season with salt and black pepper.
3. Roll out the puff pastry on the griddle and spread the onion-tomato mixture evenly on top. Cook for 5 minutes until puff pastry is golden and crispy. Remove, cut into squares, and serve warm.

15. Warm Potato and Green Bean Salad

Prep time	Cooking time	Servings
10 mins	20 mins	4

Ingredients:

- 1 lb. baby potatoes, halved
- 2 cups green beans, trimmed
- 3 tbsp olive oil
- 2 tbsp red wine vinegar
- 1 tsp Dijon mustard
- 1 tsp salt
- 1 tsp black pcpper

Tips: For quicker cooking, you can pre-boil potatoes for a few minutes before placing them on the griddle. Add a sprinkle of fresh herbs like parsley or dill for extra flavor.

Serving size: 1 cup

Nutritional values (per serving): Calories: 180; Fat: 10g; Carbs: 20g; Protein: 3g

Directions:

1. Preheat the outdoor gas griddle to medium-high heat. Drizzle olive oil on the griddle and add baby potatoes. Cook for 15 minutes until tender and golden brown.
2. Add green beans to the griddle during the last 5 minutes of cooking potatoes.
3. In a small bowl, whisk red wine vinegar, Dijon mustard, salt, and black pepper. Transfer cooked potatoes and green beans to a bowl and toss with the dressing while still warm.

16. Cauliflower Steaks with Chimichurri Sauce

Prep time	Cooking time	Servings
10 mins	15 mins	4

Ingredients:

- 1 large head of cauliflower, sliced into 4 steaks
- 1/4 cup olive oil
- Salt and pepper to taste
- 1 cup fresh parsley, chopped
- 2 tbsp fresh oregano, chopped
- 3 cloves garlic, minced
- 1/4 cup red wine vinegar

Tips: Use a flat spatula to handle the cauliflower steaks gently to avoid breaking them apart.

Serving size: 1 steak

Nutritional values (per serving): Calories: 165; Fat: 14g; Carbs: 10g; Protein: 3g

Directions:

1. Preheat the outdoor gas griddle to medium-high heat. Brush both sides of the cauliflower steaks with olive oil and season with salt and pepper.
2. Place the cauliflower steaks on the griddle and cook for 6-8 minutes on each side, until tender.
3. Meanwhile, prepare the chimichurri sauce by combining parsley, oregano, garlic, red wine vinegar, remaining olive oil, and red pepper flakes in a bowl.
4. Serve each cauliflower steak with a generous spoonful of chimichurri sauce on top.

17. Grilled Bell Pepper and Halloumi Salad

Prep time	Cooking time	Servings
10 mins	10 mins	4

Ingredients:

- 2 large bell peppers (any color), sliced into strips
- 8 oz Halloumi cheese, sliced
- 2 tbsp olive oil
- Salt and pepper to taste
- 1 tbsp balsamic vinegar

Tips: Make sure not to overcook Halloumi as it can become rubbery. Serve immediately while halloumi is warm.

Serving size: 1 cup

Nutritional values (per serving): Calories: 220; Fat: 18g; Carbs: 7g; Protein: 12g

Directions:

1. Preheat the outdoor gas griddle to medium-high heat. Toss bell pepper strips with olive oil and season with salt and pepper.
2. Place bell pepper strips on one side of the griddle and halloumi slices on the other side. Cook the bell peppers for about 5 until slightly charred and tender.
3. Cook halloumi slices for 2-3 minutes per side until golden brown.
4. Combine grilled bell peppers and halloumi in a serving bowl, then drizzle with balsamic vinegar.

18. Griddled Brussels Sprouts with Bacon

Prep time	Cooking time	Servings
10 mins	15 mins	4

Ingredients:

- 4 cups Brussels sprouts, halved
- 6 slices bacon, chopped
- 1 tbsp olive oil
- 1 tsp garlic powder
- 1/2 tsp black pepper
- 1/4 tsp salt

Tips: Ensure Brussels sprouts are evenly coated with oil for better caramelization.

Serving size: 1 cup

Nutritional values (per serving): Calories: 180; Fat: 12g; Carbs: 10g; Protein: 6g

Directions:

1. Preheat the outdoor gas griddle to medium-high heat. Add bacon to the griddle and cook until crispy. Remove and set aside.
2. Add olive oil to the bacon drippings on the griddle. Place halved Brussels sprouts on the griddle, cut-side down. Cook for 5-7 minutes until golden brown.
3. Sprinkle garlic powder, black pepper, and salt over the Brussels sprouts. Stir and cook for another 5-7 minutes until tender. Mix in the cooked bacon and serve.

19. Veggie-Stuffed Portobello Mushrooms

Prep time	Cooking time	Servings
10 mins	15 mins	4

Ingredients:

- 4 large Portobello mushrooms
- 1 cup cherry tomatoes, quartered
- 1 cup spinach, chopped
- 1/2 cup shredded mozzarella cheese
- 2 tbsp olive oil
- 1 tsp Italian seasoning
- 1/4 tsp salt

Tips: Do not overstuff mushrooms to ensure even cooking.

Serving size: 1 stuffed mushroom

Nutritional values (per serving): Calories: 150; Fat: 10g; Carbs: 8g; Protein: 8g

Directions:

1. Preheat the outdoor gas griddle to medium-high heat. Clean mushroom caps and remove stems, brushing with olive oil on both sides.
2. Place mushroom caps on the griddle, gill-side down, and cook for about 5 minutes. Flip mushrooms over and fill with cherry tomatoes and spinach.
3. Sprinkle Italian seasoning and salt over the vegetables. Top each mushroom cap with mozzarella cheese.
4. Cook for an additional 5-7 minutes until mushrooms are tender and cheese is melted.

20. Charred Eggplant Parmesan

Prep time	Cooking time	Servings
10 mins	15 mins	4

Ingredients:

- 1 large eggplant, sliced into 1/2 inch rounds
- 1 cup marinara sauce
- 1 cup shredded mozzarella cheese
- 1/4 cup grated Parmesan cheese
- 2 tbsp olive oil
- 1/2 tsp salt
- 1/2 tsp black pepper

Tips: Use a grill press or heavy pan to press down on eggplant slices for even cooking.

Serving size: 2 slices

Nutritional values (per serving): Calories: 220; Fat: 12g; Carbs: 15g; Protein: 12g

Directions:

1. Preheat your outdoor gas griddle to medium-high heat. Brush eggplant slices with olive oil and season with salt and pepper.
2. Place eggplant slices on the griddle and cook for 5 minutes on each side until charred. Spread a spoonful of marinara sauce over each slice.
3. Sprinkle mozzarella cheese evenly over the eggplant slices. Close the griddle lid to melt the cheese for 3-5 minutes. Once the cheese is melted, sprinkle Parmesan cheese on top.

21. Grilled Asparagus with Lemon-Garlic Butter

Prep time	Cooking time	Servings
5 mins	10 mins	4

Ingredients:

- 1 lb. asparagus, trimmed
- 3 tbsp butter
- 1 tbsp lemon juice
- 2 garlic cloves, minced
- Salt & black pepper to taste

Tips: Trim the woody ends of asparagus for more tender bites.

Serving size: 1/4 lb.

Nutritional values (per serving): Calories: 80; Fat: 7g; Carbs: 5g; Protein: 2g

Directions:

1. Preheat your outdoor gas griddle to medium heat. In a small saucepan, melt butter on the griddle alongside asparagus.
2. Add garlic to the melted butter and cook for 1 minute until fragrant. Toss asparagus in lemon juice, then place on the griddle.
3. Grill asparagus for 5 minutes, turning frequently until tender-crisp. Brush grilled asparagus with lemon-garlic butter and season with salt and pepper.

22. Zucchini Fritters with Yogurt Sauce

Prep time	Cooking time	Servings
20 mins	10 mins	4

Ingredients:

- 2 cups grated zucchini
- 1/4 cup all-purpose flour
- 2 tbsp grated Parmesan cheese
- 1 egg, beaten
- Salt and pepper to taste
- Olive oil for frying
- 1 cup plain Greek yogurt
- 1 tbsp lemon juice
- 1 garlic clove, minced

Tips: Squeeze out excess moisture from grated zucchini before mixing to ensure crispy fritters.

Serving size: 2 fritters

Nutritional values (per serving): Calories: 100; Fat: 6g; Carbs: 9g; Protein: 5g

Directions:

1. Preheat the outdoor gas griddle to medium-high heat and lightly grease with olive oil.
2. In a bowl, combine zucchini, flour, Parmesan cheese, egg, salt, and pepper until well mixed. Drop spoonfuls of the zucchini batter onto the griddle and flatten slightly.
3. Cook fritters for 4–5 minutes on each side or until golden brown and crispy.
4. In another bowl, combine Greek yogurt, lemon juice, and garlic to prepare the yogurt sauce. Serve hot fritters with a dollop of yogurt sauce on top.

23. Grilled Artichokes with Lemon Aioli

Prep time	Cooking time	Servings
10 mins	15 mins	4

Ingredients:

- 4 large artichokes, cleaned and halved
- 1/4 cup olive oil
- 2 tbsp lemon juice
- 1 tsp salt
- 1 tsp black pepper
- 1 cup mayonnaise
- 2 cloves garlic, minced
- 1 tsp lemon zest

Tips: For better flavor, marinate artichokes in olive oil mixture for at least an hour before grilling.

Serving size: 1 artichoke half with lemon aioli

Nutritional values (per serving): Calories: 180; Fat: 15g; Carbs: 9g; Protein: 3g

Directions:

1. Preheat the outdoor gas griddle on medium-high heat. In a large bowl, toss artichoke halves with olive oil, lemon juice, salt, and pepper.
2. Place artichokes on the griddle, cut side down, and grill for 10 minutes until charred and tender. Flip artichokes and cook for another 5 minutes.
3. Meanwhile, mix mayonnaise, garlic, and lemon zest in a small bowl to make the aioli. Serve the grilled artichokes with a dollop of lemon aioli.

24. Spicy Griddled Okra with Creole Seasoning

Prep time	Cooking time	Servings
20 mins	10 mins	4

Ingredients:

- 1 lb. fresh okra, trimmed
- 2 tbsp olive oil
- 2 tsp Creole seasoning
- 1/2 tsp salt
- Juice of one lemon

Tips: Use freshly ground black pepper along with Creole seasoning for an extra kick.

Serving size: 1 cup cooked okra

Nutritional values (per serving): Calories: 90; Fat: 7g; Carbs: 7g; Protein: 1g

Directions:

1. Preheat the outdoor gas griddle on medium-high heat. In a large bowl, toss okra with olive oil, Creole seasoning, and salt until well-coated.
2. Place okra in a single layer on the hot griddle. Cook for 8 to 10 minutes, turning occasionally until okra is tender and slightly charred.
3. Squeeze fresh lemon juice over the cooked okra before serving.

Wraps, Burger, and Sandwiches

25. Classic Beef Burger with Cheddar Cheese

Prep time	Cooking time	Servings
10 mins	15 mins	4

Ingredients:

- 1 lb. ground beef
- 1 tsp salt
- 1/2 tsp black pepper
- 4 slices cheddar cheese
- 4 burger buns
- 1/2 cup lettuce, shredded
- 1/2 cup tomato, sliced

Tips: For added flavor, try seasoning the patties with garlic powder or onion powder.

Serving size: 1 burger

Nutritional values (per serving): Calories: 450; Fat: 23g; Carbs: 28g; Protein: 30g

Directions:

1. Preheat the outdoor gas griddle to medium-high heat. Season ground beef with salt and black pepper, then form into 4 patties.
2. Grill patties on the griddle for 5-6 minutes per side. Place a slice of cheddar cheese on each patty during the last minute of cooking to melt.
3. Toast burger buns on the griddle for 1 minute until golden brown. Assemble burgers by placing each patty onto a bun and topping with lettuce and tomato.

26. Turkey and Avocado Club Sandwich

Prep time	Cooking time	Servings
10 mins	8 mins	2

Ingredients:

- 4 slices whole wheat bread
- 1 lb. turkey breast, thinly sliced
- 1 avocado, sliced
- 4 slices bacon
- 4 tomato slices
- 2 tbsp mayonnaise
- Salt and pepper to taste

Tips: To enhance flavor, you can add a slice of cheese or a handful of fresh spinach leaves.

Serving size: 1 sandwich

Nutritional values (per serving): Calories: 450; Fat: 25g; Carbs: 30g; Protein: 30g

Directions:

1. Preheat the outdoor gas griddle to medium heat. Cook the bacon for 5 minutes until crispy, then set aside.
2. Toast the bread slices on the griddle for 2 minutes on each side or until golden brown. Spread mayonnaise on one side of each toasted slice.
3. Layer turkey slices, avocado, bacon, and tomato onto two of the bread slices. Season with salt and pepper to taste. Top with the remaining two bread slices. Press down gently and serve.

27. Teriyaki Pineapple Chicken Burger

Prep time	Cooking time	Servings
10 mins	10 mins	4

Ingredients:

- 1 lb. ground chicken
- 4 pineapple rings
- 4 whole wheat burger buns
- 1/4 cup teriyaki sauce
- Lettuce leaves
- Salt and pepper to taste

Tips: Trim the woody ends of asparagus for more tender bites.

Serving size: 1/4 lb.

Nutritional values (per serving): Calories: 80; Fat: 7g; Carbs: 5g; Protein: 2g

Directions:

1. Preheat the outdoor gas griddle to medium-high heat. Mix ground chicken with salt and pepper in a bowl and form into four patties.
2. Cook patties on the griddle for 5 minutes per side. Brush teriyaki sauce onto each patty during the last minute of cooking.
3. Grill pineapple rings for 2 minutes per side until caramelized. Toast burger buns on the griddle for about 1 minute or until slightly crispy.
4. Place each patty on a bun, topped with a grilled pineapple ring and lettuce leaf.

28. BBQ Pulled Pork Sandwich

Prep time	Cooking time	Servings
20 mins	10 mins	4

Ingredients:

- 2 cups pulled pork
- 1 cup BBQ sauce
- 4 hamburger buns
- 1 cup coleslaw mix
- 2 tbsp mayonnaise

Tips: You can use pre-cooked pulled pork to save time. For extra flavor, add a few pickle slices.

Serving size: 1 sandwich

Nutritional values (per serving): Calories: 450; Fat: 15g; Carbs: 55g; Protein: 18g

Directions:

1. Preheat the outdoor gas griddle on medium-high heat. Mix the pulled pork with BBQ sauce and place it on the griddle.
2. Cook for 10 minutes, stirring occasionally until heated through. In a bowl, combine coleslaw mix and mayonnaise.
3. Toast hamburger buns on the griddle for 2 minutes. Place a generous amount of pulled pork on each bun, topped with coleslaw.

29. Spicy Black Bean Veggie Burger

Prep time	Cooking time	Servings
10 mins	15 mins	4

Ingredients:

- 2 cups black beans, drained and rinsed
- 1/2 cup breadcrumbs
- 1 egg
- 1 tsp cumin
- 1/2 tsp chili powder
- 4 hamburger buns
- Lettuce leaves

Tips: Use a spatula to press down gently on the patties while cooking for even browning.

Serving size: 1 burger

Nutritional values (per serving): Calories: 300; Fat: 6g; Carbs: 50g; Protein: 12g

Directions:

1. Preheat the outdoor gas griddle on medium-high heat. In a bowl, mash the black beans until mostly smooth. Mix in breadcrumbs, egg, cumin, and chili powder until well combined.
2. Form into four patties and place on the griddle. Cook for 5 minutes per side until browned.
3. Toast hamburger buns on the griddle for about 2 minutes. Assemble burgers with patties and lettuce leaves.

30. Greek Gyro Wrap with Tzatziki Sauce

Prep time	Cooking time	Servings
15 mins	10 mins	4

Ingredients:

- 1 lb. chicken breast, thinly sliced
- 2 tbsp olive oil
- 1 tsp garlic powder
- 1 cup Greek yogurt
- 1 cucumber, grated
- 2 tsp lemon juice
- Salt and pepper to taste

Tips: Serve with tomato and red onion slices for extra flavor.

Serving size: 1 wrap

Nutritional values (per serving): Calories: 350; Fat: 15g; Carbs: 30g; Protein: 25g

Directions:

1. Preheat the outdoor gas griddle to medium-high heat. In a bowl, mix chicken, olive oil, garlic powder, salt, and pepper.
2. Cook the chicken on the griddle for 5 minutes on each side until fully cooked.
3. Meanwhile, mix Greek yogurt, grated cucumber, lemon juice, salt, and pepper in a bowl to make the tzatziki sauce.
4. Once the chicken is done, assemble wraps with cooked chicken and tzatziki sauce in pita bread.

31. Philly Cheesesteak Sandwich

Prep time	Cooking time	Servings
10 mins	10 mins	4

Ingredients:

- 2 lbs. ribeye steak, thinly sliced
- 1 cup green bell peppers, thinly sliced
- 1 cup onions, thinly sliced
- 4 hoagie rolls
- 8 slices provolone cheese
- 2 tbsp vegetable oil
- Salt and pepper to taste

Tips: Freeze the ribeye steak slightly before slicing for easier handling.

Serving size: 1 sandwich

Nutritional values (per serving): Calories: 650; Fat: 34g; Carbs: 38g; Protein: 42g

Directions:

1. Preheat the outdoor gas griddle to medium-high heat. Add the vegetable oil to the griddle and sauté the bell peppers and onions for 5 minutes until softened.
2. Push the vegetables to the side and add the ribeye steak to the griddle. Cook for 3-5 minutes until the steak is browned. Season with salt and pepper.
3. Mix the steak with the sautéed vegetables on the griddle. Divide the steak and veggie mixture into four portions on the griddle and top each portion with two slices of provolone cheese.
4. Allow the cheese to melt before placing each portion into a hoagie roll.

32. Spicy Black Bean Veggie Burger

Prep time	Cooking time	Servings
15 mins	10 mins	4

Ingredients:

- 2 cups black beans, drained and mashed
- 1/2 cup breadcrumbs
- 1/4 cup minced onions
- 1 tsp chili powder
- 1 tsp cumin powder
- Salt and pepper to taste
- 4 burger buns
- Optional toppings (lettuce, tomatoes, avocado)

Tips: Add a dash of hot sauce to the bean mixture for extra spice.

Serving size: 1 burger

Nutritional values (per serving): Calories: 310; Fat: 8g; Carbs: 48g; Protein: 12g

Directions:

1. Preheat the outdoor gas griddle to medium heat. In a large bowl, combine mashed black beans, breadcrumbs, minced onions, chili powder, cumin powder, salt, and pepper.
2. Form mixture into four equal-sized patties. Place patties on preheated griddle and cook for 5 minutes per side or until golden brown.
3. Toast burger buns on the griddle if desired. Place each patty on a bun and add your favorite toppings.

33. Grilled Chicken Caesar Wrap

Prep time	Cooking time	Servings
10 mins	12 mins	4

Ingredients:

- 1 lb. chicken breast, thinly sliced
- 1/2 tsp salt
- 1/4 tsp black pepper
- 4 large flour tortillas
- 1/2 cup Caesar dressing
- 2 cups Romaine lettuce, chopped
- 1/4 cup grated Parmesan cheese

Tips: For extra flavor, marinate chicken in Caesar dressing for at least an hour before grilling.

Serving size: 1 wrap

Nutritional values (per serving): Calories: 350; Fat: 15g; Carbs: 15g; Protein: 34g

Directions:

1. Preheat the outdoor gas griddle to medium heat. Season chicken breast slices with salt and black pepper.
2. Grill chicken on the griddle for 5-6 minutes per side or until fully cooked. Warm tortillas on the griddle for about a minute each side.
3. Spread Caesar dressing evenly over each tortilla. Top with grilled chicken, Romaine lettuce, and grated Parmesan cheese. Roll up each tortilla tightly to form wraps.

34. Fish Tacos Wrap with Lime Crema

Prep time	Cooking time	Servings
10 mins	10 mins	4

Ingredients:

- 1 lb. white fish fillets (such as tilapia or cod)
- 1 tbsp olive oil
- 1 tsp paprika
- 1/2 tsp garlic powder
- Salt and pepper to taste
- 8 small flour tortillas
- 1/2 cup shredded cabbage
- 1/4 cup chopped cilantro

For Lime Crema:

- 1/2 cup sour cream
- Juice of 1 lime
- Zest of 1 lime

Tips: Try using different types of white fish for variety.

Serving size: 2 tacos

Nutritional values (per serving): Calories: 320; Fat: 15g; Carbs: 28g; Protein: 20g

Directions:

1. Preheat the outdoor gas griddle to medium heat. Brush the fish fillets with olive oil and season with paprika, garlic powder, salt, and pepper.
2. Cook the fish on the griddle for 3-4 minutes per side until fully cooked. Meanwhile, mix the sour cream, lime juice, and lime zest in a small bowl to make the lime crema.
3. Once the fish is done, warm the tortillas on the griddle for about 30 seconds per side.
4. Place pieces of fish on each tortilla, topping with cabbage and cilantro. Drizzle with lime crema.

Poultry Recipes

35. Herb-Marinated Chicken Breast

Prep time	Cooking time	Servings
10 mins	15 mins	4

Ingredients:

- 1 lb. chicken breast
- 1/4 cup olive oil
- 2 tbsp lemon juice
- 2 cloves garlic, minced
- 2 tsp dried oregano
- 1 tsp dried thyme
- Salt and pepper to taste

Tips: For a richer flavor, marinate the chicken for up to an hour.

Serving size: 1 chicken breast

Nutritional values (per serving): Calories: 220; Fat: 11g; Carbs: 2g; Protein: 27g

Directions:

1. In a bowl, mix olive oil, lemon juice, garlic, oregano, thyme, salt, and pepper to make the marinade. Add the chicken breasts and let it sit for at least 10 minutes.
2. Preheat your outdoor gas griddle to medium-high heat. Place the marinated chicken breasts on the griddle and cook for 7 minutes per side or until fully cooked.

36. Honey Mustard Turkey Cutlets

Prep time	Cooking time	Servings
10 mins	12 mins	4

Ingredients:

- 1 lb. turkey cutlets
- 1/4 cup honey
- 3 tbsp Dijon mustard
- Salt and pepper to taste
- 1 tbsp olive oil + more for griddle

Tips: Make sure not to overcook turkey as it can become dry.

Serving size: 1 turkey cutlet

Nutritional values (per serving): Calories: 190; Fat: 6g; Carbs: 17g; Protein: 20g

Directions:

1. Combine honey, Dijon mustard, olive oil, salt, and pepper in a bowl to make the glaze. Preheat your outdoor gas griddle to medium-high heat and lightly oil the surface.
2. Brush turkey cutlets with half of the honey-mustard glaze. Place turkey cutlets on the griddle and cook for 6 minutes per side. Brush with remaining glaze during cooking.

37. Griddled Chicken Fajitas

Prep time	Cooking time	Servings
10 mins	10 mins	4

Ingredients:

- 1 lb. boneless chicken breast, cut into strips
- 1 bell pepper, sliced
- 1 onion, sliced
- Juice from one lime
- 2 tbsp olive oil
- Salt and pepper to taste
- Flour tortillas (8-inch)

Tips: Serve with salsa or guacamole for added flavor.

Serving size: 1 fajita

Nutritional values (per serving): Calories: 295; Fat: 12g; Carbs: 28g; Protein: 22g

Directions:

1. In a bowl, mix chicken strips with lime juice, olive oil, salt, and pepper. Preheat your outdoor gas griddle to medium-high heat.
2. Place chicken strips on one side of the griddle and vegetables on the other side. Cook both for 10 minutes while stirring occasionally until chicken is fully cooked. Serve with warmed tortillas.

38. Lemon Garlic Grilled Chicken

Prep time	Cooking time	Servings
10 mins	15 mins	4

Ingredients:

- 4 boneless skinless chicken breasts (about 1 lb.)
- Juice of 2 lemons
- Zest of 1 lemon
- 2 tbsp olive oil
- 3 cloves garlic, minced
- Salt and pepper to taste

Tips: Marinate chicken longer for more intense flavor.

Serving size: 1 chicken breast

Nutritional values (per serving): Calories: 210; Fat: 9g; Carbs: 2g; Protein: 31g

Directions:

1. Preheat the outdoor gas griddle to medium-high heat. In a bowl, mix lemon juice, zest, olive oil, garlic, salt, and pepper. Marinate chicken breasts in it for at least 5 minutes.
2. Place chicken on your griddle and cook for 7 minutes per side or until fully cooked. Remove and let it rest for a couple of minutes before serving.

39. Mediterranean Grilled Chicken Kebabs

Prep time	Cooking time	Servings
10 mins	12 mins	4

Ingredients:

- 1 lb. boneless, skinless chicken breast, cut into 1-inch cubes
- 1 cup cherry tomatoes
- 1 red onion, cut into chunks
- 1 yellow bell pepper, cut into chunks
- 2 tbsp olive oil
- 2 tsp dried oregano
- 1 tsp garlic powder
- Salt and pepper to taste

Tips: Serve with a side of tzatziki sauce for extra flavor.

Serving size: 2 kebabs

Nutritional values (per serving): Calories: 250; Fat: 12g; Carbs: 10g; Protein: 24g

Directions:

1. Preheat the outdoor gas griddle to medium-high heat. In a large bowl, combine olive oil, oregano, garlic powder, salt, and pepper.
2. Add chicken, cherry tomatoes, red onion, and yellow bell pepper to the bowl and toss to coat. Thread chicken and vegetables onto skewers alternately.
3. Place skewers on your griddle and cook for 10 minutes, turning occasionally, until chicken is cooked through.

40. Buffalo Glazed Chicken Wings

Prep time	Cooking time	Servings
10 mins	12 mins	4

Ingredients:

- 2 lbs. chicken wings
- 1/4 cup buffalo hot sauce
- 2 tbsp butter, melted
- Salt and pepper to taste
- Celery sticks (optional)

Tips: For extra crispiness, pat the wings dry with paper towels before cooking.

Serving size: 5 wings

Nutritional values (per serving): Calories: 300; Fat: 20g; Carbs: 2g; Protein: 28g

Directions:

1. Preheat the outdoor gas griddle to medium-high heat. Season the chicken wings with salt and pepper. Place wings on your griddle and cook for 20 minutes, turning occasionally until crispy.
2. In a small bowl, mix melted butter and buffalo hot sauce together. Toss cooked wings in the buffalo sauce mixture until well coated. Serve with celery sticks if desired.

41. Teriyaki Chicken Thighs

Prep time	Cooking time	Servings
10 mins	15 mins	4

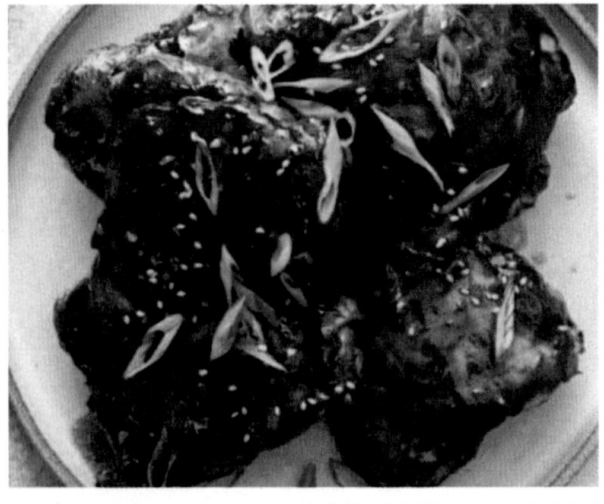

Ingredients:

- 1 lb. chicken thighs (boneless, skinless)
- 1/2 cup teriyaki sauce
- 2 tbsp olive oil
- 1/4 cup chopped green onions
- 1 tsp sesame seeds
- 1 tsp minced garlic

Tips: Use a meat thermometer to ensure the chicken reaches an internal temp of 165°F for safety.

Serving size: 1 thigh

Nutritional values (per serving): Calories: 250; Fat: 15g; Carbs: 8g; Protein: 23g

Directions:

1. Preheat the outdoor gas griddle to medium-high heat. In a bowl, mix chicken thighs with teriyaki sauce and garlic. Marinate for at least 5 minutes.
2. Brush the griddle with olive oil. Place the chicken thighs on the griddle and cook for 7 minutes on each side until caramelized.
3. Sprinkle with green onions and sesame seeds before serving.

42. Sweet and Sour Turkey Stir-Fry

Prep time	Cooking time	Servings
10 mins	12 mins	4

Ingredients:

- 1 lb. turkey breast, sliced thin
- 1/2 cup sweet and sour sauce
- 2 tbsp vegetable oil
- 1 red bell pepper, sliced
- 1 green bell pepper, sliced
- 1 medium onion, sliced

Tips: For extra crunch, add a handful of cashews at the end.

Serving size: 1/4 of total stir-fry

Nutritional values (per serving): Calories: 220; Fat: 9g; Carbs: 11g; Protein: 22g

Directions:

1. Preheat the outdoor gas griddle to medium-high heat. In a bowl, toss turkey slices with sweet and sour sauce. Set aside.
2. Brush the griddle with vegetable oil, then add bell peppers and onions, then cook for 5 minutes until slightly tender.
3. Add marinated turkey slices cook for 6-7 minutes, stirring frequently until cooked through. Mix everything together on the griddle for even flavor distribution.

43. Italian-Style Turkey Sausage Patties

Prep time	Cooking time	Servings
10 mins	15 mins	4

Ingredients:

- 1 lb. ground turkey
- 1 tbsp Italian seasoning
- 1 tsp garlic powder
- 1 tsp onion powder
- 1/2 tsp salt
- 1/2 tsp black pepper
- 2 tbsp olive oil

Tips: Serve with grilled vegetables or in a sandwich for a complete meal.

Serving size: 2 patties

Nutritional values (per serving): Calories: 220; Fat: 14g; Carbs: 1g; Protein: 21g

Directions:

1. In a bowl, mix ground turkey, Italian seasoning, garlic powder, onion powder, salt, and black pepper. Divide the mixture into 8 and shape into patties.
2. Preheat the outdoor gas griddle to medium-high heat and add olive oil. Cook patties on the griddle for 6-7 minutes per side or until browned.

44. Thai Peanut Chicken Skewers

Prep time	Cooking time	Servings
10 mins	12 mins	4

Ingredients:

- 1 lb. chicken breast, cut into chunks
- 1/4 cup peanut butter
- 2 tbsp soy sauce
- 2 tbsp lime juice
- 1 tbsp honey
- 1 tsp ground ginger

Tips: Pair with a side of jasmine rice or grilled vegetables.

Serving size: 3 skewers

Nutritional values (per serving): Calories: 270; Fat: 14g; Carbs: 8g; Protein: 27g

Directions:

1. In a bowl, mix peanut butter, soy sauce, lime juice, honey, and ground ginger to make the marinade. Add chicken chunks into the marinade and coat evenly.
2. Thread marinated chicken onto skewers. Preheat the outdoor gas griddle to medium-high heat. Cook skewers on the griddle for 12-15 minutes, turning occasionally until chicken is lightly charred.

Scan this QR code to access the exclusive Bonuses

Beef Recipes

45. Grilled Beef Steaks with Herb Butter

Prep time	Cooking time	Servings
10 mins	10 mins	4

Ingredients:

- 2 lbs. beef steaks
- 1/2 cup unsalted butter, softened
- 2 tbsp fresh parsley, chopped
- 1 tsp fresh rosemary, chopped
- 1 tsp fresh thyme, chopped
- 1 tsp garlic powder
- Salt and pepper to taste

Tips: Let the steaks rest after cooking to retain their juices.

Serving size: 1 steak

Nutritional values (per serving): Calories: 530; Fat: 40g; Carbs: 1g; Protein: 40g

Directions:

1. Mix the butter with parsley, rosemary, thyme, and garlic powder in a bowl until well combined. Preheat your outdoor gas griddle to medium-high heat.
2. Season the beef steaks generously with salt and pepper. Place the steaks on the griddle and cook for 4-5 minutes per side or until desired doneness.
3. Remove the steaks and let rest for a few minutes. Top each steak with a dollop of herb butter before serving.

46. Teriyaki Grilled Beef Skewers

Prep time	Cooking time	Servings
10 mins	15 mins	4

Ingredients:

- 2 lbs. beef sirloin, cut into cubes
- 1/2 cup soy sauce
- 1/4 cup honey
- 2 tbsp rice vinegar
- 1 tsp garlic powder

Tips: Brush leftover marinade onto skewers while grilling for added flavor.

Serving size: 3 skewers

Nutritional values (per serving): Calories: 320; Fat: 12g; Carbs: 20g; Protein: 32g

Directions:

1. In a large bowl, combine soy sauce, honey, rice vinegar, and garlic powder to make the teriyaki marinade. Add beef cubes and let sit for at least 30 minutes.
2. Preheat your outdoor gas griddle to medium-high heat. Thread the marinated beef onto soaked wooden skewers.
3. Place skewers on the griddle and cook for 3-4 minutes per side or until fully cooked through.

47. Pepper-Crusted Beef Medallions

Prep time	Cooking time	Servings
10 mins	8 mins	4

Ingredients:

- 1 lb. beef tenderloin, cut into medallions
- 2 tbsp cracked black pepper
- 2 tsp sea salt
- 1 tbsp olive oil
- 2 tbsp butter
- 1 clove garlic, minced

Tips: Press the pepper lightly into the meat for maximum flavor.

Serving size: 2 medallions

Nutritional values (per serving): Calories: 320; Fat: 22g; Carbs: 1g; Protein: 28g

Directions:

1. Season beef medallions with cracked black pepper and sea salt. Heat olive oil and butter on the outdoor gas griddle over medium-high heat.
2. Add garlic to the griddle and sauté until fragrant. Place medallions on the griddle and cook for 4 minutes on each side for medium-rare.

48. Honey Sriracha Beef Kabobs

Prep time	Cooking time	Servings
10 mins	12 mins	4

Ingredients:

- 1 lb. beef sirloin, cut into 1-inch cubes
- 2 tbsp honey
- 2 tbsp sriracha sauce
- 1 tbsp soy sauce
- 1 tbsp vegetable oil
- 1 red onion, cut into chunks
- 1 bell pepper, cut into chunks

Tips: Adjust the amount of sriracha to control the spice level.

Serving size: 1 skewer

Nutritional values (per serving): Calories: 250; Fat: 12g; Carbs: 10g; Protein: 25g

Directions:

1. Preheat your outdoor gas griddle to medium-high heat. In a bowl, combine honey, sriracha sauce, soy sauce, and vegetable oil.
2. Thread the beef cubes, onion, and bell pepper onto skewers. Brush the honey-sriracha mixture over the skewers.
3. Place the skewers on the griddle and cook for 8-10 minutes, turning occasionally.

49. Bacon-Wrapped Griddled Sirloin

Prep time	Cooking time	Servings
10 mins	15 mins	4

Ingredients:

- 4 sirloin steaks (5 oz each)
- 8 slices of bacon
- Salt and pepper to taste

Tips: Use thick-cut bacon for a juicier wrap. Remove toothpicks before serving.

Serving size: 1 steak

Nutritional values (per serving): Calories: 350; Fat: 22g; Carbs: 0g; Protein: 35g

Directions:

1. Preheat your outdoor gas griddle to medium-high heat. Season each sirloin steak with salt and pepper.
2. Wrap two slices of bacon around each steak and secure with toothpicks if needed. Place the steaks on the griddle and cook for 6-7 minutes per side or until bacon is crispy.

50. Korean BBQ Beef (Bulgogi)

Prep time	Cooking time	Servings
15 mins	10 mins	4

Ingredients:

- 1 lb. beef ribeye, thinly sliced
- 1/4 cup soy sauce
- 2 tbsp sugar
- 1 tbsp sesame oil
- 1 tbsp minced garlic
- 1/2 tsp ground black pepper
- 1/4 cup sliced green onions

Tips: Serve with steamed rice or lettuce wraps. Garnish with sesame seeds for added flavor.

Serving size: 4 oz.

Nutritional values (per serving): Calories: 290; Fat: 15g; Carbs: 8g; Protein: 28g

Directions:

1. In a bowl, mix soy sauce, sugar, sesame oil, minced garlic, and black pepper. Add the sliced beef and green onions to the marinade. Let it sit for at least 15 minutes.
2. Preheat the outdoor gas griddle on medium-high heat. Cook the marinated beef on the griddle for 5-7 minutes until it's browned and cooked through, stirring occasionally.

51. Beer-Marinated Grilled Carne Asada

Prep time	Cooking time	Servings
10 mins	10 mins	4

Ingredients:

- 1 lb. flank steak
- 1 cup beer
- 2 tbsp lime juice
- 2 tbsp soy sauce
- 1 tsp cumin
- 2 cloves garlic, minced
- Salt and pepper to taste

Tips: Serve with tortillas and your favorite toppings like cilantro and onions.

Serving size: 4 oz.

Nutritional values (per serving): Calories: 320; Fat: 12g; Carbs: 3g; Protein: 45g

Directions:

1. In a bowl, combine beer, lime juice, soy sauce, cumin, garlic, salt, and pepper. Marinate the flank steak in the mixture for at least an hour.
2. Preheat the outdoor gas griddle on medium-high heat. Remove steak and grill for 5 minutes on each side or until desired doneness.

52. Thai Basil Griddled Beef Stir-Fry

Prep time	Cooking time	Servings
10 mins	10 mins	4

Ingredients:

- 1 lb. beef sirloin, thinly sliced
- 1 cup Thai basil leaves
- 2 tbsp soy sauce
- 1 tbsp fish sauce
- 2 cloves garlic, minced
- 1 tsp brown sugar
- Salt and pepper to taste

Tips: Serve over jasmine rice or noodles.

Serving size: 4 oz.

Nutritional values (per serving): Calories: 290; Fat: 15g; Carbs: 4g; Protein: 25g

Directions:

1. Preheat the outdoor gas griddle on medium-high heat. Add beef slices to the griddle and cook until browned. Add garlic and cook for another minute.
2. Stir in soy sauce, fish sauce, and brown sugar until well combined. Mix in Thai basil leaves and cook until wilted.

53. Blackened Cajun Beef Tips with Peppers and Onions

Prep time	Cooking time	Servings
10 mins	15 mins	4

Ingredients:

- 1 lb. beef tips
- 2 tbsp olive oil
- 1 tbsp Cajun seasoning
- 1 bell pepper, sliced
- 1 onion, sliced
- Salt and pepper to taste

Tips: Serve hot off the griddle for best flavor.

Serving size: 1 cup

Nutritional values (per serving): Calories: 320; Fat: 18g; Carbs: 10g; Protein: 30g

Directions:

1. Preheat the outdoor gas griddle to medium-high heat. Toss beef tips with olive oil and Cajun seasoning.
2. Cook the beef tips on the griddle for 5 minutes until browned. Add bell pepper and onion slices, then cook for another 10 minutes until vegetables are tender. Season with salt and pepper to taste.

54. Grilled Beef and Pineapple Teriyaki Bowls

Prep time	Cooking time	Servings
10 mins	20 mins	4

Ingredients:

- 1 lb. beef sirloin, sliced
- 1 cup teriyaki sauce
- 2 cups pineapple chunks
- 1 bell pepper, sliced
- 1 tbsp sesame oil

Tips: Serve over cooked rice for a complete meal.

Serving size: 1 bowl

Nutritional values (per serving): Calories: 350; Fat: 10g; Carbs: 35g; Protein: 25g

Directions:

1. Preheat the outdoor gas griddle to medium-high heat. In a bowl, marinate the beef slices with half of the teriyaki sauce for at least 5 minutes.
2. Grill beef on the griddle for 8 minutes or until cooked through. Add pineapple chunks and bell pepper to the griddle, then cook for another 5 minutes.
3. Combine everything on the griddle and drizzle remaining teriyaki sauce over it

55. Ribeye Steaks with Garlic Mushrooms

Prep time	Cooking time	Servings
10 mins	12 mins	4

Ingredients:

- 2 lbs. ribeye steak (two steaks)
- Salt and pepper to taste
- 2 tbsp olive oil
- 8 oz. mushrooms, sliced
- 2 tbsp butter
- 1 tsp minced garlic

Tips: Let steaks rest for a few minutes before slicing to keep juices in.

Serving size: 8 oz. of steak with mushrooms

Nutritional values (per serving): Calories: 450; Fat: 35g; Carbs: 4g; Protein: 28g

Directions:

1. Preheat the outdoor gas griddle on high heat. Season the ribeye steaks with salt and pepper. Place steaks on the griddle and cook for 5-6 minutes per side for medium rare.
2. Meanwhile, add olive oil to one side of the griddle and sauté mushrooms until soft. Add butter and garlic to mushrooms for the last couple of minutes of cooking.
3. Serve steak topped with garlic mushrooms.

56. Indian Spiced Beef Kebabs

Prep time	Cooking time	Servings
10 mins	20 mins	4

Ingredients:

- 1 lb. ground beef
- 2 tbsp garam masala
- 1 tsp turmeric powder
- 1 tsp cumin powder
- 1 tsp coriander powder
- 1 tbsp minced garlic
- Salt and pepper to taste

Tips: Ensure to mix the spices thoroughly for even flavor distribution.

Serving size: 2 kebabs

Nutritional values (per serving): Calories: 250; Fat: 15g; Carbs: 2g; Protein: 25g

Directions:

1. In a bowl, combine ground beef with garam masala, turmeric, cumin, coriander, garlic, salt, and pepper. Mix well and shape the mixture into kebabs.
2. Preheat the outdoor gas griddle on medium-high heat. Cook the kebabs for 5 minutes on each side or until fully cooked. Serve hot with your favorite dipping sauce.

Pork Recipes

57. Grilled Honey Garlic Pork Chops

Prep time	Cooking time	Servings
10 mins	15 mins	4

Ingredients:

- 4 pork chops (1 inch thick)
- 3 tbsp honey
- 3 cloves garlic, minced
- 1/4 cup soy sauce
- 1 tbsp apple cider vinegar
- 1/2 tsp black pepper

Tips: Baste the pork chops with leftover marinade while grilling for extra flavor.

Serving size: 1 pork chop

Nutritional values (per serving): Calories: 280; Fat: 10g; Carbs: 17g; Protein: 28g

Directions:

1. In a bowl, mix honey, garlic, soy sauce, apple cider vinegar, and black pepper. Marinate pork chops in the mixture for at least an hour.
2. Preheat the outdoor gas griddle to medium-high heat. Grill pork chops for 6-7 minutes per side or until they reach an internal temperature of 145°F.
3. Remove and let it rest for a few minutes.

58. Smoky BBQ Pork Ribs

Prep time	Cooking time	Servings
15 mins	30 mins	4

Ingredients:

- 2 lbs. baby back pork ribs
- 1 cup BBQ sauce
- 1 tbsp smoked paprika
- 1 tsp garlic powder
- 1 tsp onion powder
- Salt and pepper to taste

Tips: For extra smoky flavor, consider using a smoke box or smoke chips on your gas griddle.

Serving size: 1/2 lb. ribs

Nutritional values (per serving): Calories: 250; Fat: 14g; Carbs: 12g; Protein: 20g

Directions:

1. Preheat the outdoor gas griddle to medium heat. Season the ribs with smoked paprika, garlic powder, onion powder, salt, and pepper.
2. Place the ribs on the griddle and cook for 25 minutes, turning occasionally. Brush the ribs with BBQ sauce during the last 5 minutes of cooking.

59. Lemon Herb Pork Tenderloins

Prep time	Cooking time	Servings
10 mins	20 mins	4

Ingredients:

- 1 lb. pork tenderloin
- Zest and juice of 1 lemon
- 2 tbsp olive oil
- 1 tsp dried rosemary
- 1 tsp dried thyme
- Salt and pepper to taste

Tips: Allow the pork to marinate in lemon herb mixture for a more intense flavor.

Serving size: 4 oz tenderloin

Nutritional values (per serving): Calories: 220; Fat: 10g; Carbs: 3g; Protein: 27g

Directions:

1. Preheat the outdoor gas griddle to medium-high heat. In a small bowl, combine lemon zest, juice, olive oil, rosemary, thyme, salt, and pepper.
2. Rub the mixture onto the pork tenderloin evenly. Place the tenderloin on the griddle and cook for 20 minutes, turning occasionally. Remove and let rest for a few minutes before slicing.

60. Teriyaki Glazed Pork Skewers

Prep time	Cooking time	Servings
15 mins	15 mins	4

Ingredients:

- 1 lb. pork loin, cut into cubes
- 1/2 cup teriyaki sauce
- 2 tbsp honey
- Salt and pepper to taste

Tips: Soaking wooden skewers prevents them from burning during cooking.

Serving size: Two skewers

Nutritional values (per serving): Calories: 250; Fat: 7g; Carbs: 16g; Protein: 29g

Directions:

1. Preheat the outdoor gas griddle to medium-high heat. In a small bowl, combine teriyaki sauce and honey. Thread pork cubes onto soaked wooden skewers.
2. Season lightly with salt and pepper. Place skewers on the griddle and cook for 12-15 minutes, turning occasionally. Brush with teriyaki glaze during the last few minutes of cooking.

61. Lime Marinated Pork Steaks

Prep time	Cooking time	Servings
10 mins	15 mins	4

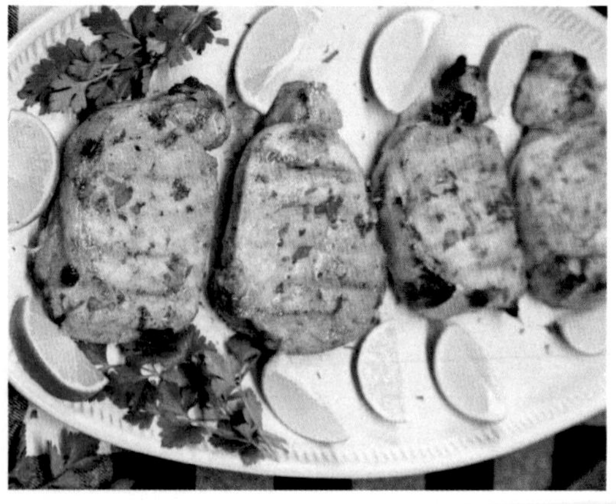

Ingredients:

- 4 pork steaks (about 1 lb. each)
- 1/4 cup lime juice
- 2 tbsp olive oil
- 2 tsp garlic powder
- 1 tsp salt
- 1/2 tsp black pepper
- 1 tsp ground cumin

Tips: For extra flavor, garnish with fresh cilantro and lime wedges.

Serving size: 1 pork steak

Nutritional values (per serving): Calories: 280; Fat: 15g; Carbs: 2g; Protein: 32g

Directions:

1. In a bowl, combine lime juice, olive oil, garlic powder, salt, black pepper, and ground cumin.
2. Add the pork steaks, mix well and marinate for at least 30 minutes or up to 4 hours in the refrigerator.
3. Preheat your outdoor gas griddle to medium-high heat.
4. Remove pork steaks from marinade and place on the hot griddle. Cook for about 7 minutes on each side or until internal temperature reaches 145°F.

62. Mustard Herb-Crusted Pork Ribs

Prep time	Cooking time	Servings
15 mins	25 mins	4

Ingredients:

- 2 lbs. pork ribs
- 1/4 cup Dijon mustard
- 2 tbsp olive oil
- 2 tsp dried rosemary
- 2 tsp dried thyme
- 1 tsp garlic powder
- Salt and pepper to taste

Tips: Serve with a side of coleslaw or grilled vegetables for a complete meal.

Serving size: 8 oz.

Nutritional values (per serving): Calories: 450; Fat: 28g; Carbs: 3g; Protein: 40g

Directions:

1. Preheat your outdoor gas griddle to medium heat. In a small bowl, mix Dijon mustard, olive oil, rosemary, thyme, garlic powder, salt, and pepper.
2. Spread the mustard herb mixture evenly over both sides of the ribs. Place ribs on the preheated griddle.
3. Cook for 12 minutes per side or until ribs are nicely browned. Let the ribs rest for a few minutes before slicing and serving.

63. Maple Dijon Grilled Pork Medallions

Prep time	Cooking time	Servings
10 mins	15 mins	4

Ingredients:

- 1 lb. pork tenderloin, cut into medallions
- 1/4 cup maple syrup
- 3 tbsp Dijon mustard
- 2 tbsp soy sauce
- 1 tbsp olive oil
- 1 tsp garlic powder
- Salt and pepper to taste

Tips: Serve with grilled vegetables or a fresh salad for a complete meal.

Serving size: 1 medallion

Nutritional values (per serving): Calories: 200; Fat: 6g; Carbs: 12g; Protein: 24g

Directions:

1. Preheat the outdoor gas griddle to medium-high heat. In a small bowl, mix together maple syrup, Dijon mustard, soy sauce, olive oil, garlic powder, salt, and pepper.
2. Brush the pork medallions with the marinade and let sit for 5 minutes. Place the pork medallions on the griddle and cook for 7-8 minutes per side until fully cooked through.
3. Remove and let rest for a few minutes before serving.

64. Caribbean Jerk Griddled Pork Chops

Prep time	Cooking time	Servings
10 mins	20 mins	4

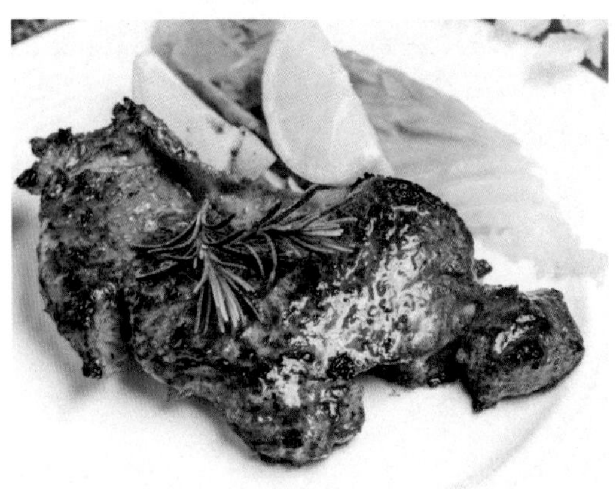

Ingredients:

- 4 pork chops (about 1 lb. total)
- 3 tbsp Caribbean jerk seasoning
- 2 tbsp olive oil
- Juice of one lime
- Salt and pepper to taste

Tips: Pair with grilled pineapple or mango salsa for an authentic Caribbean flavor.

Serving size: 1 pork chop

Nutritional values (per serving): Calories: 250; Fat: 10g; Carbs: 4g; Protein: 34g

Directions:

1. Preheat the outdoor gas griddle to medium-high heat. In a small bowl, combine Caribbean jerk seasoning, olive oil, lime juice, salt, and pepper.
2. Rub the spice mixture all over the pork chops. Place the pork chops on the griddle and cook for about 10 minutes per side or until cooked through.

65. Mediterranean Stuffed Pork Loin

Prep time	Cooking time	Servings
15 mins	30 mins	4

Ingredients:

- 1 ½-lb. pork loin
- 1/2 cup spinach, chopped
- 1/4 cup sun-dried tomatoes, chopped
- 1/4 cup feta cheese, crumbled
- 2 tbsp olive oil
- 1 tsp dried oregano
- Salt and pepper to taste

Tips: Use toothpicks to keep the stuffing in place if needed.

Serving size: 4 oz.

Nutritional values (per serving): Calories: 290; Fat: 16g; Carbs: 4g; Protein: 31g

Directions:

1. Preheat the outdoor gas griddle to medium-high heat. Cut a slit through the center of the pork loin to create a pocket.
2. In a bowl, combine spinach, sun-dried tomatoes, feta cheese, oregano, salt, and pepper. Stuff the mixture into the pork loin pocket.
3. Rub the pork loin with olive oil, salt, and pepper on all sides. Place the pork loin on the griddle and cook for 15 minutes per side or until the internal temperature reaches 145°F.

66. Sweet and Sour Griddled Pork

Prep time	Cooking time	Servings
10 mins	20 mins	4

Ingredients:

- 1 ½-lb. pork tenderloin, sliced into medallions
- 1/2 cup pineapple juice
- 1/4 cup apple cider vinegar
- 1/4 cup brown sugar
- 2 tbsp soy sauce
- Salt and pepper to taste

Tips: Serve over rice for a more filling meal. Garnish with green onions for added flavor.

Serving size: 5 medallions

Nutritional values (per serving): Calories: 320; Fat: 8g; Carbs: 12g; Protein: 36g

Directions:

1. Preheat the outdoor gas griddle to medium-high heat.
2. In a bowl, mix pineapple juice, apple cider vinegar, brown sugar, soy sauce, salt, and pepper to make the sauce. Season pork medallions with salt and pepper.
3. Place the medallions on the hot griddle and cook for 5 minutes per side until browned. Pour sauce over medallions and cook for an additional minute until glazed.

Lamb Recipes

67. Griddled Lamb Chops with Rosemary

Prep time	Cooking time	Servings
10 mins	8 mins	4

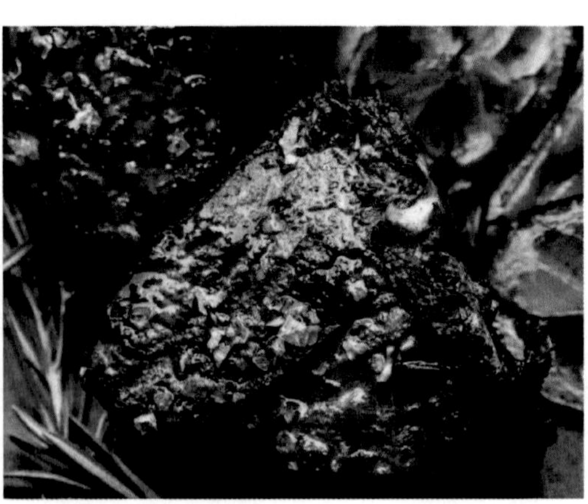

Ingredients:

- 1 ½-lb. lamb chops
- 2 tbsp olive oil
- 2 tsp dried rosemary
- 1 tsp salt
- 1/2 tsp black pepper
- 4 cloves garlic, minced

Tips: For best results, allow the lamb chops to come to room temperature before cooking.

Serving size: 1 lamb chop

Nutritional values (per serving): Calories: 250; Fat: 20g; Carbs: 2g; Protein: 16g

Directions:

1. Preheat your outdoor gas griddle to medium-high heat. In a bowl, combine olive oil, rosemary, salt, black pepper, and garlic.
2. Coat the lamb chops with the mixture and let them marinate for at least 10 minutes. Place lamb chops on the hot griddle; cook for 4 minutes on each side or until desired doneness.

68. Spicy Marinated Lamb Skewers

Prep time	Cooking time	Servings
15 mins	10 mins	4

Ingredients:

- 1 ½-lb. pork tenderloin, sliced into medallions
- 1/2 cup pineapple juice
- 1/4 cup apple cider vinegar
- 1/4 cup brown sugar
- 2 tbsp soy sauce
- Salt and pepper to taste

Tips: Serve with a cooling yogurt dip if desired.

Serving size: 4 cubes of lamb

Nutritional values (per serving): Calories: 275; Fat:15g; Carbs: 4g; Protein: 26g

Directions:

1. Preheat your outdoor gas griddle to medium-high heat. In a bowl, mix olive oil, lemon juice, garlic, chili powder, cumin, salt, and pepper.
2. Add lamb cubes to the marinade, then let sit for at least 15 minutes. Thread marinated lamb onto skewers.
3. Cook skewers on the hot griddle for 10 minutes, turning frequently until cooked through.

69. Lemon Herb Griddled Lamb Steaks

Prep time	Cooking time	Servings
10 mins	15 mins	4

Ingredients:

- 2 lbs. lamb steaks
- 1/4 cup olive oil
- 2 tbsp lemon juice
- 2 tsp dried oregano
- 2 tsp dried rosemary
- 3 garlic cloves, minced
- Salt and pepper to taste

Tips: Serve with grilled vegetables or a fresh salad for a complete meal.

Serving size: 1 steak

Nutritional values (per serving): Calories: 360; Fat: 22g; Carbs: 3g; Protein: 37g

Directions:

1. In a bowl, combine olive oil, lemon juice, oregano, rosemary, garlic, salt, and pepper. Coat the lamb steaks with the mixture and let marinate for at least 30 minutes.
2. Preheat your outdoor gas griddle to medium-high heat. Cook the lamb steaks for 6-7 minutes per side, or until desired doneness.

70. Teriyaki Glazed Lamb Ribs

Prep time	Cooking time	Servings
15 mins	30 mins	4

Ingredients:

- 2 lbs. lamb ribs
- 1/2 cup teriyaki sauce
- 3 tbsp honey
- 1 tsp ground ginger
- Salt and pepper to taste

Tips: Baste with remaining marinade while cooking for extra flavor.

Serving size: 8 ribs

Nutritional values (per serving): Calories: 420; Fat: 28g; Carbs: 20g; Protein: 26g

Directions:

1. Season the lamb ribs with salt and pepper. In a small bowl, mix teriyaki sauce, honey, and ground ginger. Coat the ribs with it and let marinate for at least an hour.
2. Preheat your outdoor gas griddle to medium heat. Cook the lamb ribs for 15 minutes per side or until caramelized.

71. Herb Crusted Rack of Lamb

Prep time	Cooking time	Servings
10 mins	25 mins	4

Ingredients:

- 1 rack of lamb (about 2 lb.)
- 1/4 cup breadcrumbs
- 2 tbsp olive oil
- 2 tsp dried rosemary
- 2 tsp dried thyme
- Salt and pepper to taste

Tips: Pair with a mint yogurt sauce for added flavor.

Serving size: 3 ribs

Nutritional values (per serving): Calories: 420; Fat: 34g; Carbs: 6g; Protein: 18g

Directions:

1. Preheat your outdoor gas griddle to medium heat. In a small bowl, mix breadcrumbs, olive oil, rosemary, thyme, salt, and pepper.
2. Coat the rack of lamb with the breadcrumb mixture pressing firmly to adhere. Place the rack on the griddle meat-side down and cook for 10 minutes or until browned.
3. Flip and cook for another 15 minutes or until desired doneness is achieved. Remove and let rest for a few minutes before slicing.

72. Mint and Yogurt Marinated Lamb Kebabs

Prep time	Cooking time	Servings
15 mins	30 mins	4

Ingredients:

- 1 lb. lamb, cut into 1-inch cubes
- 1 cup plain yogurt
- 2 tbsp fresh mint, chopped
- 1 tsp cumin powder
- 1 tbsp lemon juice
- 1 tsp salt
- 1/2 tsp black pepper

Tips: Soak wooden skewers in water for about 30 minutes to prevent them from burning.

Serving size: 2 skewers

Nutritional values (per serving): Calories: 220; Fat: 10g; Carbs: 7g; Protein: 25g

Directions:

1. In a mixing bowl, combine yogurt, mint, cumin powder, lemon juice, salt, and black pepper. Add lamb cubes to the mixture and toss to coat evenly.
2. Marinate in the refrigerator for at least 30 minutes. Preheat griddle to medium-high heat. Thread marinated lamb onto skewers.
3. Cook on the griddle for about 12-15 minutes or until done, turning occasionally.

73. Indian Spiced Lamb Seekh Kebabs

Prep time	Cooking time	Servings
20 mins	15 mins	4

Ingredients:

- 1 lb. ground lamb
- 2 tbsp fresh cilantro, chopped
- 1 tsp ground coriander
- 1 tsp garam masala
- 1/2 tsp ground turmeric
- 1 tbsp lemon juice
- Salt to taste

Tips: Serve with a squeeze of fresh lemon juice and a side of mint chutney.

Serving size: 2 kebabs

Nutritional values (per serving): Calories: 270; Fat: 18g; Carbs: 3g; Protein: 22g

Directions:

1. In a bowl, combine ground lamb with cilantro, coriander, garam masala, turmeric, lemon juice, and salt. Shape mixture into long sausage-like shapes and thread onto skewers.
2. Preheat griddle to medium-high heat. Cook kebabs on the griddle for 12-15 minutes or until done, turning occasionally.

74. Moroccan Spiced Ground Lamb Patties

Prep time	Cooking time	Servings
10 mins	12 mins	4

Ingredients:

- 1 lb. ground lamb
- 2 tsp ground cumin
- 2 tsp ground coriander
- 1 tsp ground cinnamon
- 1/2 tsp ground allspice
- 1/4 cup finely chopped onion
- Salt and pepper to taste

Tips: Serve with a side of tzatziki sauce and flatbread for a complete meal.

Serving size: 1 patty

Nutritional values (per serving): Calories: 230; Fat: 18g; Carbs: 2g; Protein: 15g

Directions:

1. Preheat your outdoor gas griddle to medium-high heat. In a bowl, combine the ground lamb, cumin, coriander, cinnamon, allspice, chopped onion, salt, and pepper.
2. Form the mixture into patties. Cook the patties on the griddle for about 5-6 minutes on each side or until fully cooked.

75. Mediterranean Lamb Meatballs

Prep time	Cooking time	Servings
10 mins	25 mins	4

Ingredients:

- 1 lb. ground lamb
- 1/4 cup breadcrumbs
- 2 tbsp chopped fresh parsley
- 2 cloves garlic, minced
- 1 tsp dried oregano
- Salt and pepper to taste
- Olive oil for cooking

Tips: Enjoy with a Greek salad or hummus for extra flavor.

Serving size: 4 meatballs

Nutritional values (per serving): Calories: 250; Fat: 20g; Carbs: 5g; Protein: 16g

Directions:

1. Preheat your outdoor gas griddle to medium heat. In a bowl, combine the ground lamb, breadcrumbs, parsley, garlic, oregano, salt, and pepper.
2. Form the mixture into small meatballs. Grease the griddle with a little olive oil. Cook the meatballs on the griddle for 8-10 minutes, turning occasionally until they are evenly browned.

76. BBQ Grilled Lamb Spare Ribs

Prep time	Cooking time	Servings
15 mins	30 mins	4

Ingredients:

- 2 lbs. lamb spare ribs
- 1/2 cup BBQ sauce
- 1 tbsp olive oil
- 2 tsp garlic powder
- 2 tsp smoked paprika
- Salt and pepper to taste

Tips: For an extra smoky flavor, use smoked BBQ sauce.

Serving size: 4 oz.

Nutritional values (per serving): Calories: 350; Fat: 28g; Carbs: 6g; Protein: 20g

Directions:

1. Preheat your outdoor gas griddle to medium-high heat. Rub the lamb spare ribs with olive oil, garlic powder, smoked paprika, salt, and pepper.
2. Place the ribs on the griddle and cook for 15 minutes on each side or until browned. Brush the ribs with BBQ sauce during the last 5 minutes of cooking.

Fish and Seafood

77. Garlic Butter Shrimp Skewers

Prep time	Cooking time	Servings
10 mins	5 mins	4

Ingredients:

- 1 lb. large shrimp, peeled and deveined
- 3 tbsp butter, melted
- 2 cloves garlic, minced
- 1 tsp paprika
- 1 tsp dried parsley
- 1/2 tsp salt
- 1/4 tsp black pepper

Tips: Serve with a lemon wedge for added flavor.

Serving size: 4 shrimp skewers

Nutritional values (per serving): Calories: 160; Fat: 8g; Carbs: 2g; Protein: 22g

Directions:

1. Preheat your outdoor gas griddle to medium-high heat. In a bowl, combine melted butter, minced garlic, paprika, dried parsley, salt, and black pepper.
2. Thread shrimp onto skewers and brush with the garlic butter mixture. Place shrimp skewers on the griddle and cook for 2-3 minutes on each side until shrimp is pink and opaque.

78. Lemon Herb Grilled Salmon

Prep time	Cooking time	Servings
10 mins	12 mins	4

Ingredients:

- 4 salmon fillets (6 oz. each)
- 3 tbsp olive oil
- 1 lemon, juiced and zested
- 1 tbsp fresh dill or parsley, chopped
- 2 cloves garlic, minced
- 1/2 tsp salt
- 1/4 tsp black pepper

Tips: For extra zest, sprinkle additional lemon zest over cooked salmon before serving.

Serving size: 1 salmon fillet

Nutritional values (per serving): Calories: 310; Fat: 21g; Carbs: 2g; Protein: 28g

Directions:

1. Preheat your outdoor gas griddle to medium-high heat. In a small bowl, combine olive oil, lemon juice and zest, dill or parsley, garlic, salt, and black pepper.
2. Brush the salmon fillets with the lemon herb mixture. Place the salmon fillets skin-side down on the griddle and cook for 5-6 minutes per side or until fully cooked.

79. Teriyaki Tuna Steaks

Prep time	Cooking time	Servings
10 mins	5 mins	4

Ingredients:

- 4 tuna steaks (1 lb.)
- 1/4 cup teriyaki sauce
- 2 tbsp olive oil
- 2 tsp sesame seeds
- 1 tsp grated ginger

Tips: Serve with a side of grilled vegetables for a complete meal.

Serving size: 1 tuna steak

Nutritional values (per serving): Calories: 300; Fat: 14g; Carbs: 6g; Protein: 38g

Directions:

1. Preheat the outdoor gas griddle to high heat. Brush tuna steaks with teriyaki sauce and let them sit for a few minutes.
2. Drizzle olive oil on the griddle and cook tuna steaks for 3-4 minutes on each side until seared outside but pink in the center.
3. Sprinkle sesame seeds and grated ginger over cooked tuna steaks.

80. Citrus Garlic Butter Broiled Oysters

Prep time	Cooking time	Servings
10 mins	12 mins	4

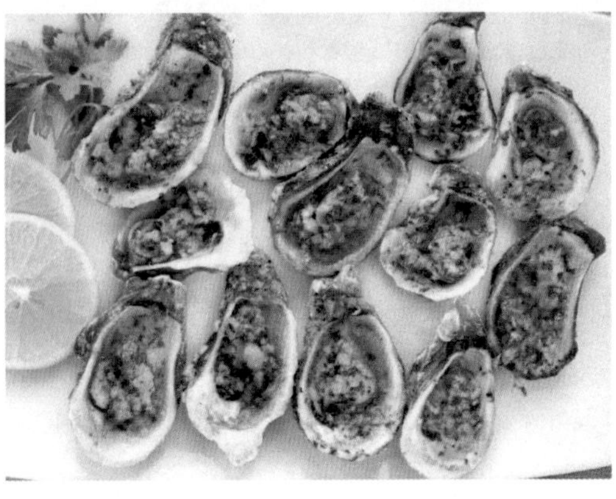

Ingredients:

- 2 dozen oysters, shucked
- 1/2 cup unsalted butter, melted
- 1 tbsp garlic, minced
- 2 tbsp lemon juice
- 1 tbsp parsley, chopped
- 1/2 tsp salt
- 1/4 tsp black pepper

Tips: Use fresh oysters for optimal flavor.

Serving size: 6 oysters

Nutritional values (per serving): Calories: 190; Fat: 16g; Carbs: 3g; Protein: 7g

Directions:

1. Preheat your outdoor gas griddle to medium-high heat. In a small mixing bowl, combine melted butter, garlic, lemon juice, parsley, salt, and black pepper.
2. Arrange shucked oysters on the griddle. Spoon the butter mixture over each oyster. Broil for 3-5 minutes or until the edges of the oysters curl and they are cooked through.

81. Teriyaki Glazed Salmon Kebabs

Prep time	Cooking time	Servings
15 mins	10 mins	4

Ingredients:

- 1 lb. salmon fillet, cut into cubes
- 1/4 cup teriyaki sauce
- 1 tbsp olive oil
- 1 red bell pepper, cut into chunks
- 1 yellow bell pepper, cut into chunks

Tips: Use fresh salmon for better flavor and texture.

Serving size: 1 kebab

Nutritional values (per serving): Calories: 220; Fat: 11g; Carbs: 8g; Protein: 24g

Directions:

1. Preheat the outdoor gas griddle to medium-high heat. In a bowl, combine the salmon cubes and teriyaki sauce.
2. Thread the salmon and bell peppers onto skewers, alternating pieces. Brush with olive oil and place on the griddle.
3. Cook for about 8-10 minutes, turning occasionally, until salmon is cooked through.

82. Grilled Mahi Mahi with Pineapple Salsa

Prep time	Cooking time	Servings
15 mins	10 mins	4

Ingredients:

- 4 mahi mahi fillets (about 1 lb.)
- Salt and pepper to taste
- 1 cup pineapple, diced
- 1/2 cup red bell pepper, diced
- 1/4 cup red onion, finely chopped
- 2 tbsp fresh cilantro, chopped
- 2 tbsp lime juice

Tips: For additional flavor, marinate the mahi mahi in lime juice and olive oil for 30 minutes before cooking.

Serving size: 1 fillet with salsa

Nutritional values (per serving): Calories: 220; Fat: 4g; Carbs: 12g; Protein: 32g

Directions:

1. Preheat your outdoor gas griddle to medium-high heat. Season the mahi mahi fillets with salt and pepper.
2. Place the mahi mahi on the griddle and cook for 4-5 minutes on each side until it flakes easily.
3. Meanwhile, prepare the pineapple salsa by combining the pineapple, red bell pepper, red onion, cilantro, and lime juice in a bowl.
4. Remove the mahi mahi and serve with some pineapple salsa on top.

83. Shrimp Scampi Pizza

Prep time	Cooking time	Servings
10 mins	15 mins	4

Ingredients:

- 1 lb. large shrimp, peeled and deveined
- 1 pre-made pizza crust
- 1/4 cup olive oil
- 3 cloves garlic, minced
- 1/2 cup shredded mozzarella cheese
- Lemon zest from one lemon

Tips: Pre-cook shrimp to ensure they are fully cooked through on the pizza.

Serving size: 2 slices

Nutritional values (per serving): Calories: 350; Fat: 18g; Carbs: 27g; Protein: 20g

Directions:

1. Preheat the outdoor gas griddle to medium heat. In a skillet over the griddle, heat olive oil and sauté garlic until fragrant.
2. Add shrimp to the skillet and cook for 3-4 minutes until pink. Brush the pizza crust with some of the garlic-infused oil. Spread shrimp evenly on top of the crust.
3. Sprinkle with mozzarella cheese and lemon zest. Place pizza on the griddle and cook for 10 minutes, or until the crust is crispy and cheese is melted.

84. Thai Chili Garlic Prawns

Prep time	Cooking time	Servings
10 mins	8 mins	4

Ingredients:

- 1 lb. large prawns, peeled and deveined
- 2 tbsp olive oil
- 3 cloves garlic, minced
- 2 tbsp Thai sweet chili sauce
- Salt to taste
- Juice of one lime

Tips: Serve these prawns over steamed rice or noodles for a complete meal.

Serving size: 4 prawns

Nutritional values (per serving): Calories: 170; Fat: 6g; Carbs: 6g; Protein: 22g

Directions:

1. Preheat your outdoor gas griddle to medium-high heat. In a small bowl, whisk together olive oil, minced garlic, Thai sweet chili sauce, and lime juice.
2. Toss the prawns in the marinade until well coated. Place the prawns on the griddle and cook for 3-4 minutes on each side until they turn pink. Season with salt to taste before serving.

85. Mediterranean Griddled Octopus Salad

Prep time	Cooking time	Servings
15 mins	10 mins	4

Ingredients:

- 1 lb. octopus, cleaned and cut into pieces
- 2 cups mixed greens
- 1/2 cup cherry tomatoes, halved
- 1/4 cup red onion, thinly sliced
- 2 tbsp olive oil
- 1 tbsp lemon juice
- 1 tsp dried oregano
- Salt and pepper to taste

Tips: Ensure the griddle is hot before adding the octopus to achieve a good sear.

Serving size: 1 cup of salad

Nutritional values (per serving): Calories: 230; Fat: 14g; Carbs: 8g; Protein: 18g

Directions:

1. Preheat the outdoor gas griddle to medium-high heat. Toss the octopus pieces with 1 tbsp olive oil, oregano, salt, and pepper.
2. Place the octopus on the griddle and cook for 5-7 minutes until charred and tender.
3. In a large bowl, combine the mixed greens, cherry tomatoes, and red onion. In a small bowl, whisk together the remaining olive oil and lemon juice.
4. Add the grilled octopus to the salad and drizzle with the dressing. Toss gently to coat and serve.

86. Grilled Lobster Tails with Garlic Butter Sauce

Prep time	Cooking time	Servings
10 mins	15 mins	4

Ingredients:

- 4 lobster tails (about 6 oz each)
- 1/4 cup butter, melted
- 3 cloves garlic, minced
- 2 tbsp lemon juice
- Salt and pepper to taste

Tips: For extra flavor, garnish with freshly chopped parsley.

Serving size: 1 lobster tail

Nutritional values (per serving): Calories: 240; Fat: 15g; Carbs: 2g; Protein: 22g

Directions:

1. Preheat the outdoor gas griddle to medium heat. Using kitchen shears, cut the top shell of each lobster tail lengthwise down the middle and pull apart slightly to expose the meat.
2. In a small bowl, mix butter, garlic, lemon juice, salt, and pepper. Brush lobster tails with the garlic butter mixture.
3. Place lobster tails flesh side down on the griddle and cook for 5-7 minutes until slightly charred. Flip them over and continue cooking for another 5-7 minutes until meat is opaque.
4. Brush again with garlic butter sauce just before serving.

87. Honey Soy Glazed Swordfish Steak

Prep time	Cooking time	Servings
10 mins	10 mins	4

Ingredients:

- 1/4 cup honey
- 1/4 cup soy sauce
- 2 tbsp olive oil
- 1 tbsp lemon juice
- 1 tsp garlic powder
- 4 swordfish steaks (6 oz each)
- Salt and pepper to taste

Tips: To prevent sticking, make sure the griddle is hot before placing swordfish on it.

Serving size: 1 steak

Nutritional values (per serving): Calories: 320; Fat: 12g; Carbs: 16g; Protein: 35g

Directions:

1. In a bowl, mix honey, soy sauce, olive oil, lemon juice, and garlic powder. Season swordfish steaks with salt and pepper.
2. Preheat the outdoor gas griddle to medium-high heat. Brush the griddle with a little oil. Place swordfish steaks on the griddle.
3. Cook for about 4 minutes on one side, then flip. Brush the glaze mixture on top of the steaks.
4. Cook for another 4-5 minutes or until the fish is cooked through and has a nice glaze.

88. Grilled Scallops with Cilantro Lime Butter

Prep time	Cooking time	Servings
10 mins	15 mins	4

Ingredients:

- 1 lb. large scallops
- Salt and pepper to taste
- 2 tbsp butter, melted
- Zest of one lime
- Juice of one lime
- 2 tbsp chopped fresh cilantro

Tips: Make sure not to overcook the scallops as they can become tough.

Serving size: 4 oz.

Nutritional values (per serving): Calories: 140; Fat: 8g; Carbs: 3g; Protein:18g

Directions:

1. Season scallops with salt and pepper. Preheat the outdoor gas griddle to medium-high heat. Lightly grease the griddle with oil. Place scallops on the griddle.
2. Cook for 2-3 minutes on each side until opaque and slightly charred.
3. In a small bowl, mix melted butter, lime zest, lime juice, and chopped cilantro. Once scallops are done, drizzle them with cilantro lime butter.

Sweet Desserts

89. Grilled Pineapple Upside-Down Cake

Prep time	Cooking time	Servings
15 mins	10 mins	4

Ingredients:

- 1 can pineapple rings in juice (8 oz)
- 1 box yellow cake mix (use only dry mix)
- 2/3 cup brown sugar
- 1/4 cup unsalted butter, melted
- Maraschino cherries (optional)
- Vanilla ice cream (optional serving)

Tips: Ensure even cooking by rotating the skillet occasionally on the griddle.

Serving size: 1/4 of the total cake

Nutritional values (per serving): Calories: 320; Fat: 10g; Carbs: 55g; Protein: 3g

Directions:

1. Preheat your outdoor gas griddle to medium heat. In a cast iron skillet, melt the butter on the heated griddle and sprinkle brown sugar evenly over it.
2. Lay pineapple rings on top of the brown sugar mixture and place a maraschino cherry in the center of each ring if using. Evenly sprinkle dry cake mix over the pineapples.
3. Cover with a lid or foil and cook for 10 minutes until cake mix is set and slightly browned. Remove and let it cool slightly before inverting onto a serving plate.

90. Honey Grilled Peaches and Cream

Prep time	Cooking time	Servings
10 mins	8 mins	4

Ingredients:

- 4 ripe peaches, halved and pitted
- 2 tbsp honey
- 1 tbsp olive oil
- 1 cup whipped cream
- 1/2 tsp ground cinnamon

Tips: Use ripe but firm peaches for best results.

Serving size: 1 peach half with cream

Nutritional values (per serving): Calories: 120; Fat: 5g; Carbs: 18g; Protein: 1g

Directions:

1. Preheat the outdoor gas griddle to medium-high heat. Brush peach halves with olive oil and drizzle with honey. Place peaches cut side down on the griddle.
2. Grill for about 5 minutes per side until caramelized and tender. Transfer grilled peaches to a serving plate.
3. Top each peach half with some whipped cream and a sprinkle of ground cinnamon.

91. Summer Berry Tart

Prep time	Cooking time	Servings
15 mins	10 mins	4

Ingredients:

- 1 pre-made tart crust
- 2 cups mixed summer berries (strawberries, blueberries, raspberries)
- 3 tbsp sugar
- 1 tbsp lemon juice
- 1/2 cup Greek yogurt
- Fresh mint leaves (optional)

Tips: Keep an eye on the tart crust to prevent burning. Use any combination of your favorite berries.

Serving size: 1 slice

Nutritional values (per serving): Calories: 180; Fat: 6g; Carbs: 28g; Protein: 3g

Directions:

1. Preheat the outdoor gas griddle to medium heat. Roll out the tart crust and place it on a lightly oiled griddle pan. Cook the crust for 5 minutes until lightly browned, flipping once.
2. In a bowl, mix berries with sugar and lemon juice. Spread Greek yogurt over the tart crust. Top with mixed berries. Garnish with fresh mint leaves if desired.

92. Grilled Strawberry Shortcake

Prep time	Cooking time	Servings
10 mins	15 mins	4

Ingredients:

- 1 lb. fresh strawberries, sliced
- 1 cup heavy cream
- 1 tbsp sugar
- 4 shortcake biscuits
- 2 tbsp butter

Tips: Ensure to only lightly grill the biscuits for a toasty effect without burning.

Serving size: 1 shortcake

Nutritional values (per serving): Calories: 350; Fat: 22g; Carbs: 29g; Protein: 4g

Directions:

1. Preheat the outdoor gas griddle to medium heat. In a bowl, whip the heavy cream with sugar until it forms soft peaks. Split the shortcake biscuits in half.
2. Melt the butter on the griddle and place the biscuits cut-side down to grill for 2-3 minutes until golden brown.
3. Place the grilled biscuit bottom on a plate, topping with strawberries and whipped cream, then placing the biscuit top.

93. Classic Crêpe Suzette

Prep time	Cooking time	Servings
15 mins	10 mins	4

Ingredients:

- 1 cup all-purpose flour
- 2 eggs
- 1/2 cup milk
- 1/2 cup water
- 1/4 cup melted butter
- Zest of one orange
- Juice of one orange

Tips: Serve immediately to enjoy the fresh citrus flavor.

Serving size: 2 crêpes

Nutritional values (per serving): Calories: 250; Fat: 12g; Carbs: 28g; Protein: 6g

Directions:

1. Preheat the outdoor gas griddle to medium heat. In a bowl, mix flour and eggs, gradually adding milk and water until smooth. Add butter and mix well.
2. Lightly oil the griddle and pour about a quarter cup of batter onto it, spread out into a thin layer. Cook each crêpe for 1 minute per side or until golden brown.
3. In another pan on the griddle, heat orange juice with zest to make a sauce. Fold crêpes into quarters and drizzle with orange sauce.

94. Chocolate Chip Griddle Cookies

Prep time	Cooking time	Servings
10 mins	8 mins	12

Ingredients:

- 1/2 cup unsalted butter, melted
- 1/2 cup brown sugar
- 1/4 cup granulated sugar
- 1 large egg
- 1 tsp vanilla extract
- 1 1/2 cups all-purpose flour
- 1/2 tsp baking soda
- 1 cup chocolate chips

Tips: Ensure cookies are spaced apart to prevent sticking.

Serving size: 1 cookie

Nutritional values (per serving): Calories: 150; Fat: 8g; Carbs: 20g; Protein: 2g

Directions:

1. Preheat the outdoor gas griddle to medium heat. In a bowl, mix butter, brown sugar, and granulated sugar until well combined.
2. Add the egg and vanilla extract, mixing until smooth. Stir in flour and baking soda until just combined. Fold in chocolate chips.
3. Scoop tablespoon-sized portions onto the griddle, pressing down lightly to flatten. Cook for 3-4 minutes on each side or until golden brown.

95. Campfire Griddled Brownies

Prep time	Cooking time	Servings
10 mins	10 mins	8

Ingredients:

- 1/2 cup unsalted butter, melted
- 3/4 cup granulated sugar
- 2 large eggs
- 1 tsp vanilla extract
- 3/4 cup all-purpose flour
- 1/4 cup cocoa powder
- Pinch of salt

Tips: Cover the brownies with aluminum foil while cooking to retain heat.

Serving size: 1 brownie

Nutritional values (per serving): Calories: 220; Fat: 12g; Carbs: 27g; Protein: 3g

Directions:

1. Preheat the outdoor gas griddle to medium-low heat. In a bowl, combine melted butter and sugar until smooth. Add eggs and vanilla extract, mixing well.
2. Stir in flour, cocoa powder, and salt until fully incorporated. Pour batter onto a greased griddle-safe baking pan.
3. Place the pan on the griddle and cook for about 10 minutes or until brownies are set.

96. Pineapple Coconut Griddle Bread

Prep time	Cooking time	Servings
10 mins	15 mins	4

Ingredients:

- 1 cup all-purpose flour
- 2 tsp baking powder
- 2 tbsp sugar
- 1/2 cup milk
- 1/4 cup shredded coconut
- 1/2 cup crushed pineapple (drained)
- 2 tbsp butter

Tips: Flip carefully using a wide spatula to avoid breaking the bread.

Serving size: 1 piece

Nutritional values (per serving): Calories: 180; Fat: 7g; Carbs: 24g; Protein: 3g

Directions:

1. In a bowl, mix all-purpose flour, baking powder, and sugar. Stir in milk until a batter forms. Fold in shredded coconut and crushed pineapple.
2. Preheat your outdoor gas griddle to medium-low heat, then melt butter on the griddle. Pour batter into small rounds on the griddle.
3. Cook each side for about 3-4 minutes or until golden brown.

97. Griddled Banana Split

Prep time	Cooking time	Servings
5 mins	10 mins	2

Ingredients:

- 2 bananas, halved length-wise
- 1/4 cup chocolate chips
- 2 tbsp peanut butter
- Whipped cream (for top-ping)
- Maraschino cherries (op-tional)

Tips: Add maraschino cherries on top for extra flavor and color.

Serving size: 1/2 banana split

Nutritional values (per serving): Calories: 220; Fat: 10g; Carbs: 33g; Protein: 4g

Directions:

1. Preheat your outdoor gas griddle to medium heat. Place banana halves on the griddle, cut side down. Grill for about 3 minutes per side until caramelized.
2. Melt peanut butter in a microwave-safe dish. Place grilled bananas on a plate and drizzle with melted peanut butter.
3. Sprinkle chocolate chips over the top and add a dollop of whipped cream.

98. Caramelized Peach Cobbler

Prep time	Cooking time	Servings
10 mins	20 mins	4

Ingredients:

- 4 cups sliced peaches (fresh or canned, drained)
- 1 cup granulated sugar
- 1 tsp ground cinnamon
- 1/2 cup all-purpose flour
- 1/2 cup unsalted butter, melted
- 1 tsp vanilla extract
- Pinch of salt

Tips: For added crunch, sprinkle with some chopped nuts before serving.

Serving size: 1 cup

Nutritional values (per serving): Calories: 310; Fat: 14g; Carbs: 48g; Protein: 2g

Directions:

1. Preheat your outdoor gas griddle to medium heat. In a bowl, mix together the peaches, sugar, and cinnamon.
2. Spread the peach mixture evenly on the griddle and cook for 5-7 minutes until caramelized.
3. In a separate bowl, mix the flour, butter, vanilla extract, and salt until it forms a dough-like consistency. Spread dollops of the dough mixture over the caramelized peaches on the griddle.
4. Cook for an additional 10-13 minutes until the dough is golden brown.

99. Cinnamon Apple Griddle Cakes

Prep time	Cooking time	Servings
15 mins	15 mins	4

Ingredients:

- 2 cups all-purpose flour
- 2 tsp baking powder
- 2 tbsp granulated sugar
- 1 tsp ground cinnamon
- Pinch of salt
- 1 lb. apples (peeled, cored and diced)
- 1 cup milk

Tips: Cover the brownies with aluminum foil while cooking to retain heat.

Serving size: 1 brownie

Nutritional values (per serving): Calories: 220; Fat: 12g; Carbs: 27g; Protein: 3g

Directions:

1. Preheat your outdoor gas griddle to medium heat. In a large mixing bowl, combine flour, baking powder, sugar, cinnamon, and salt.
2. Gradually add milk to the dry ingredients to form a thick batter. Fold in the diced apples. Lightly grease the griddle with a bit of oil or butter.
3. Drop spoonfuls of the batter onto the griddle and cook for 2-3 minutes on each side or until golden brown. Serve hot with butter or syrup if desired.

100. Caramelized Pineapple Rings

Prep time	Cooking time	Servings
10 mins	20 mins	4

Ingredients:

- 1 fresh pineapple, cored and sliced into rings
- 1/4 cup brown sugar
- 2 tbsp butter, melted
- 1 tsp ground cinnamon

Tips: For an added flavor boost, sprinkle with a little sea salt before serving.

Serving size: 1 ring

Nutritional values (per serving): Calories: 100; Fat: 3g; Carbs: 21g; Protein: <1g

Directions:

1. Preheat your outdoor gas griddle to medium-high heat. In a small bowl, mix brown sugar, melted butter, and ground cinnamon together.
2. Brush the pineapple rings with the mixture on both sides. Place pineapple rings on the griddle and cook for 5 minutes per side or until caramelized.

30-Day Meal Plan

DAY	BREAKFAST	LUNCH	DINNER	DESSERTS
1	Breakfast Bagel Bites	Garlic Butter Shrimp Skewers	Griddled Lamb Chops with Rosemary	Grilled Pineapple Upside-Down Cake
2	Buttermilk Biscuits and Gravy	Herb-Marinated Chicken Breast	Grilled Vegetable Skewers with Herb Marinade	Caramelized Pineapple Rings
3	Huevos Rancheros Breakfast Bowls	Honey Soy Glazed Swordfish Steak	Grilled Beef Steaks with Herb Butter	Cinnamon Apple Griddle Cakes
4	Loaded Breakfast Pizza	Classic Beef Burger with Cheddar Cheese	BBQ Grilled Lamb Spare Ribs	Caramelized Peach Cobbler
5	Eggs In a Basket	Thai Peanut Chicken Skewers	Zucchini Fritters with Yogurt Sauce	Griddled Banana Split
6	Corned Beef Hash and Fried Eggs	Grilled Scallops with Cilantro Lime Butter	Teriyaki Pineapple Chicken Burger	Pineapple Coconut Griddle Bread
7	Blueberry Pancakes with Maple Syrup	Fish Tacos Wrap with Lime Crema	Mediterranean Lamb Meatballs	Campfire Griddled Brownies
8	Golden French Toast with Fresh Berries	Grilled Lobster Tails with Garlic Butter Sauce	Charred Eggplant Parmesan	Chocolate Chip Griddle Cookies
9	Bacon and Egg Breakfast Burritos	Italian-Style Turkey Sausage Patties	Thai Basil Griddled Beef Stir-Fry	Classic Crêpe Suzette
10	English Muffins with Smoked Salmon	Shrimp Scampi Pizza	Mint and Yogurt Marinated Lamb Kebabs	Grilled Strawberry Shortcake
11	Mushroom and Spinach Frittata	Grilled Chicken Caesar Wrap	Veggie-Stuffed Portobello Mushrooms	Summer Berry Tart
12	Breakfast Skillet with Sausage and Potatoes	Mediterranean Griddled Octopus Salad	Beer-Marinated Grilled Carne Asada	Honey Grilled Peaches and Cream
13	Breakfast Bagel Bites	Sweet and Sour Turkey Stir-Fry	Moroccan Spiced Ground Lamb Patties	Grilled Pineapple Upside-Down Cake
14	Buttermilk Biscuits and Gravy	Thai Chili Garlic Prawns	Caramelized Onion and Tomato Tart	Caramelized Pineapple Rings

DAY	BREAKFAST	LUNCH	DINNER	DESSERTS
15	Huevos Rancheros Breakfast Bowls	Turkey and Avocado Club Sandwich	Korean BBQ Beef (Bulgogi)	Cinnamon Apple Griddle Cakes
16	Loaded Breakfast Pizza	Grilled Mahi Mahi with Pineapple Salsa	Indian Spiced Lamb Seekh Kebabs	Caramelized Peach Cobbler
17	Eggs In a Basket	Honey Mustard Turkey Cutlets	Spicy Black Bean Veggie Burger	Griddled Banana Split
18	Corned Beef Hash and Fried Eggs	Lemon Herb Grilled Salmon	Pepper-Crusted Beef Medallions	Pineapple Coconut Griddle Bread
19	Blueberry Pancakes with Maple Syrup	Philly Cheesesteak Sandwich	Spicy Marinated Lamb Skewers	Campfire Griddled Brownies
20	Golden French Toast with Fresh Berries	Teriyaki Tuna Steaks	Cauliflower Steaks with Chimichurri Sauce	Chocolate Chip Griddle Cookies
21	Bacon and Egg Breakfast Burritos	Buffalo Glazed Chicken Wings	Honey Sriracha Beef Kabobs	Classic Crêpe Suzette
22	English Muffins with Smoked Salmon	Teriyaki Glazed Salmon Kebabs	Herb Crusted Rack of Lamb	Grilled Strawberry Shortcake
23	Mushroom and Spinach Frittata	Greek Gyro Wrap with Tzatziki Sauce	Grilled Honey Garlic Pork Chops	Summer Berry Tart
24	Breakfast Skillet with Sausage and Potatoes	Citrus Garlic Butter Broiled Oysters	Spicy Black Bean Veggie Burger	Honey Grilled Peaches and Cream
25	Breakfast Bagel Bites	Griddled Chicken Fajitas	Lemon Herb Griddled Lamb Steaks	Grilled Pineapple Upside-Down Cake
26	Buttermilk Biscuits and Gravy	BBQ Pulled Pork Sandwich	Bacon-Wrapped Griddled Sirloin	Caramelized Pineapple Rings
27	Huevos Rancheros Breakfast Bowls	Grilled Bell Pepper and Halloumi Salad	Maple Dijon Grilled Pork Medallions	Cinnamon Apple Griddle Cakes
28	Loaded Breakfast Pizza	Mediterranean Grilled Chicken Kebabs	Teriyaki Glazed Lamb Ribs	Caramelized Peach Cobbler
29	Eggs In a Basket	Warm Potato and Green Bean Salad	Mustard Herb-Crusted Pork Ribs	Griddled Banana Split
30	Corned Beef Hash and Fried Eggs	Lime Marinated Pork Steaks	Lemon Garlic Grilled Chicken	Pineapple Coconut Griddle Bread

Conclusion

Reflecting on the journey we've taken through the "Blackstone Outdoor Gas Griddle Cookbook," it's safe to say that we've covered a lot of ground. Starting from the basics of unboxing and assembling your Blackstone griddle, to advanced cooking techniques, each section has been crafted to ensure you get the most out of your griddle. The joy of cooking on a Blackstone griddle isn't just about the delicious food it helps create; it's also about the community and memories it fosters.

One cannot overemphasize the benefits of using a Blackstone griddle. It's versatile, efficient, and perfect for any meal. Whether you're flipping pancakes for breakfast or searing steaks for dinner, the griddle makes everything easier and tastier. The guide on maintenance ensures your griddle stays in top condition, allowing it to serve you well for years.

As we explored different meal ideas, it became evident that the possibilities are endless. From classic breakfast items like fluffy pancakes and crispy bacon to nutritious vegetable side dishes, wraps, burgers, and sandwiches—the variety is truly impressive. Not forgetting delectable poultry dishes, succulent beef recipes, mouth-watering pork meals, flavorful lamb preparations, and delightful fish and seafood options. And yes, even sweet treats have their place on the griddle.

The 30-day meal plan was designed to give you a seamless experience in exploring what your griddle can do. It serves as both inspiration and a practical guide in planning your meals without fuss. Using a Blackstone griddle can transform how you approach cooking—turning it into an enjoyable and fulfilling activity. You've learned not just recipes but techniques that elevate your culinary skills. But beyond these practical aspects, my final bit of advice is this: enjoy the process. Cooking should be fun and experimental. Don't be afraid to try new things or put your twist on old favorites.

Remember, outdoor gridding isn't just about feeding ourselves; it's about sharing good times with those we care about. So, fire up that Blackstone griddle often—host barbecues, enjoy family breakfasts outdoors, or simply treat yourself to an exquisite solo dinner now and then.

Food Temperature Chart

FOOD TYPE	EXAMPLE	TEMPERATURE
Breakfast Foods	Eggs (Scrambled/Fried)	300-350°F
	Omelettes	300-350°F
	Pancakes	350-375°F
	French Toast	350-375°F
	Bacon and Sausage	375-400°F
	Hashbrowns and Potatoes	375-425°F
Vegetables	Bell peppers	375-425°F
	Onions	375-425°F
	Mushrooms	350-400°F
	Green beans and peas	350-400°F
	Diced potatoes	375-425°F
	Broccoli	375-425°F
	Squash (yellow and zucchini)	350-400°F
	Asparagus	350-400°F
	Corn (kernels and on the cob)	350-400°F
	Brussel sprouts	375-425°F
Meat	Smash burgers	425-475°F
	Thicker burgers	375-425°F
	Chicken (breast/thighs)	375-400°F
	Pork chops	375-425°F
	Hot dogs	375-400°F
	Ground beef (taco)	375-425°F
	Thin steaks	450-500°F
	Thicker steaks	400-450°F
	Salmon and fish filets	350-400°F
	Shrimp	375-425°F

FOOD TYPE	EXAMPLE	TEMPERATURE
Other Griddle Foods	Fried Rice	425-475°F
	Asian Stir Fry Recipes	425-475°F
	Grilled Cheese	325-375°F
	Quesadillas/Tortillas	350-375°F
	Frozen French Fries	375-400°F
	Pasta Dishes	350-375°F

Frequently Asked Questions (FAQ)

1. What oils are best for seasoning?

A: Oils with high smoke points work best for seasoning your griddle such as vegetable oil, canola oil, flaxseed oil, and sunflower oil.

2. How can I prevent rust on my griddle top?

A: Preventing rust is key to maintaining your Blackstone griddle's longevity. The best way to prevent rust is by keeping your griddle seasoned and stored properly. After each use, clean it thoroughly using water and a scraper, then dry it completely with a cloth. Apply a thin layer of vegetable oil or any other cooking oil over the surface before storing it, which forms a protective barrier against moisture. Additionally, use a heavy-duty canvas cover to shield it from the elements when not in use.

3. How do I remove rust from my griddle top?

A: Removing rust from your griddle top requires a few steps but is simple enough to do at home. Start by scraping off any loose rust with a metal scraper. Then, use some oil and steel wool or an abrasive pad to scrub away the more stubborn areas of rust. Wipe down the surface with a cloth soaked in vinegar or lemon juice until all the rust spots are gone. Finally, rinse with water, dry completely, and re-season the griddle to restore its protective layer.

4. How should I store my griddle for extended periods?

A: If you're planning to store your griddle for an extended period, proper care is essential. Clean it thoroughly and dry it completely before applying a generous layer of oil for protection against moisture and rust. Cover your griddle well using a heavy-duty cover or store it indoors if possible.

5. Can you over-season a griddle?

A: It's tough to over-season a griddle as a heavily seasoned surface creates non-stick conditions ideal for cooking. However, excessive build-up might occur if too much oil is applied frequently without proper heating in between coats. Always heat the griddle post-oiling until smoke appears; this ensures oils polymerize into protective layers rather than building up unseasoned residue over time.

6. Tips for keeping food from sticking on a griddle?

A: Several tips will help keep food from sticking on your Blackstone Griddle:

- Ensure the surface is well-seasoned.
- Preheat the griddle properly before adding food.
- Use an appropriate amount of oil or butter.
- Avoid overcrowding; give enough room for food items so they can release moisture efficiently.
- Use utensils designed for non-stick surfaces when flipping foods.

7. How to replace/repair a Blackstone ignitor?

A: If your ignitor stops working, replacing it might be necessary. Locate the ignitor by removing control knobs and faceplate panels. Disconnect wires attached carefully noting positions. Install replacement parts following previous wire arrangements; manufacturers often offer guides/diagrams specific per model ensuring correct connections performed safely.

8. Can an olive oil cooking spray be used on the griddle before cooking?

A: Yes! Olive oil sprays are great alternatives when it comes down efficient lubrication ensuring foods fried/sautéed crispy conditions achieved every time usage starts over prepped seasoned surfaces evenly apply thin coats accordingly preferences see results experienced tried tested fans customers alike recommending this practice indeed safe good practice adopt today!

9. Can I cook tin foil meals on the griddle?

A: Yes, you can absolutely cook tin foil meals on your Blackstone griddle! Tin foil meals are a convenient and delicious way to cook multiple ingredients together. Just be sure to preheat your griddle before placing the tin foil packet on it. Cooking in tin foil helps lock in flavors and moisture, making for tasty results.

10. How do you make the best smash burgers?

A: The key to exceptional smash burgers is simplicity and technique. Start by rolling ground beef into balls about the size of a golf ball. Preheat your griddle on high heat and add a bit of oil or butter. Place the beef balls on the hot griddle and immediately press them down with a spatula for about 10 seconds. This creates a perfect sear and caramelized crust. Season with salt and pepper, flip after 2-3 minutes, cook another 1-2 minutes, and voila! Delicious smash burgers.

11. What is the best way to clean the exterior of my Blackstone?

A: Cleaning the exterior of your Blackstone is straightforward. First, ensure it's completely cool. Wipe it down with a damp cloth using mild soap if needed. For stubborn spots, a mixture of water and vinegar works great. Dry it thoroughly to prevent any rust or water spots.

12. How do you clean the burners on a Blackstone? The flames have changed colors.

A: Discolored flames can indicate blocked burners. Turn off your griddle and allow it to cool completely before cleaning. Remove the burners and use a brush or compressed air to clear out any debris or residue blocking the ports. Check for any signs of rust or damage while you're at it.

13. Tips for cooking grilled cheese on a griddle?

A: Grilled cheese on a griddle is a game changer! Butter both sides of your bread slices generously. Preheat your griddle on medium-low heat and place bread slices butter-side down until golden brown, then flip and add cheese slices between two bread pieces. Once both sides are nicely browned and the cheese has melted, you're ready to enjoy!

14. Can you bake on a Blackstone?

A: Yes, you can bake on a Blackstone! With proper accessories like baking sheets or pizza stones, you can whip up cookies, pizzas, bread, or even cakes right on your griddle. Maintain consistent low heat and monitor closely to prevent burning.

15. Can I cut food directly on the griddle?

A: It's not recommended to cut food directly on your Blackstone griddle as it might damage its surface. Use cutting boards for chopping vegetables, meats, or other ingredients.

16. Is it okay to eat off the griddle if there is rust on it?

A: It's better not to eat off a rusty griddle surface. Rust can affect both flavor and safety of food prepared this way. If you notice rust, clean it thoroughly before cooking.

Measurements And Conversions

VOLUME EQUIVALENTS (LIQUID)		
US STANDARD	US OUNCES	METRIC (APPROX.)
1 teaspoon	1/6 oz	5 ml
1 tablespoon	1/2 oz	15 ml
1 fluid ounce	1 oz	30 ml
1 cup	8 oz	240 ml
1 pint	16 oz	475 ml
1 quart	32 oz	950 ml
1 gallon	128 oz	3.8 L

VOLUME EQUIVALENTS (DRY)		WEIGHT EQUIVALENTS	
US STANDARD	METRIC (APPROX.)	US STANDARD	METRIC (APPROX.)
1/4 teaspoon	1.25 ml	1 ounce	28 g
1/2 teaspoon	2.5 ml	4 ounces	113 g
1 teaspoon	5 ml	8 ounces	225 g
1/4 cup	60 ml	12 ounces	340 g
1/3 cup	80 ml	One pound (16oz)	455 g
1/2 cup	120 ml		
1 cup	240 ml		

Made in the USA
Columbia, SC
14 December 2024

f3879a91-eddd-4622-8387-aa8ce8fd320bR01